Fig. 1. CADET COLOR GUARDS AT TUSKEGEE

Fig. 2. POST HEADQUARTERS, TUSKEGEE ARMY AIR FIELD

The Tuskegee Airmen

THE STORY OF THE NEGRO IN
THE U. S. AIR FORCE

By

CHARLES E. FRANCIS

First Lieut. U. S. Air Force (Reserve)

BOSTON
BRUCE HUMPHRIES, INC.
Publishers

Second Printing November 1968

*To My Friends of the 99th Fighter
Squadron and the 332nd Fighter Group
Who Made This Story*

ACKNOWLEDGMENTS

I wish to thank my friends of the 99th Fighter Squadron and the 332nd Fighter Group who made this story possible. In a personal sense I am deeply indebted to Mr. Leo Kerford, former Public Relations Officer of Tuskegee Army Air Field, whose cooperation and assistance enabled me to gather much of this material. I am especially grateful to my wife, who was an invaluable assistant in the preparation of this narrative. I am also deeply grateful to the following: Colonel Benjamin O. Davis, Jr., former Commanding Officer of the 99th Fighter Squadron and the 332nd Fighter Group; Mr. Vincent Brown, Professor of Political Science, Howard University; and Major Ulysses G. Lee, U. S. Army Historical Division.

CONTENTS

ILLUSTRATIONS

All Photos by U. S. Army Air Force

PREFACE

Dramatic and exciting as any adventure story ever written are the memories of every combat pilot. He may never express it in words, but every combat pilot has some particular incident indelibly fixed in his mind: lifting a wing at the last split second over a silenced flak tower, peeling off in a whistling dive to attack a roundhouse or marshalling yard, seeing the bright lines of tracers streak past as an enemy fighter comes out of the sun, hitting the deck and roaring across enemy territory at tree top level, dodging flak and small arms fire after attacking an enemy airfield, watching a locomotive speed hopelessly down the rails trying to outrun attacking planes, watching an enemy pilot throw back his canopy and bounce high out of his smoking plane, plowing through a formation of enemy fighters, getting back in friendly territory with plane torn practically apart with hardly enough gas to land, or not getting back and bailing out in unknown territory. Yes, these are but a few memories that perhaps every fighter pilot recalls when he thinks of his combat days.

This story of the part played by the Air Force cannot be told by the generals, the military analysts, the war correspondents, or even the historians, however gifted they may be. It can only be told by the pilots, crewmen, and ground complement of the U. S. Air Force—the men who actually made the history and survived. For years to come they will tell it in corner drug stores and barber shops, at home and on the streets throughout the country, wherever people talk about the war.

This narrative has a manifold purpose which has interwoven threads of deeds, actions, thoughts, and ideals into one composite story. It is the story of Negro airmen who went to war as members of the 99th Fighter Squadron and the 332nd Fighter Group as integral parts of the 12th and 15th Air

Forces. It does not pretend to be a complete historical record or an exact appraisal of what they accomplished. It does not pretend to prove that the Negro airmen who fought over Europe won the war for the allies. It simply tries to tell as accurately as possible the story of these men who fought to defend their land to the best of their abilities. The significance must not be lost, however, that it was as American citizens these men served, fought, and died in order that this nation might live to fulfill the ideals and principles of its founders—to become a haven for peoples of all races, colors, and creeds who love and cherish freedom.

CHAPTER I

THE FIGHT FOR THE RIGHT TO FIGHT

Far down in the deep south in Tuskegee, Alabama, approximately twelve miles from the famous Tuskegee Institute, stands an abandoned Army Air Field. Today this field is only a memory for thousands of Negroes throughout the United States, military and civilian, men and women, who in answer to the call of their country, came here to develop this site as a training center for Negro pilots. Today this ghost field located in a beautiful rolling valley is a desolate place. How different from the days when it was teeming with activity—with planes zooming overhead at all hours and happy, singing cadets marching to and from classes. How different from the day when the first Negro cadets were commissioned as pilots of the United States Army Air Force.

It was on March 7, 1942, that five young men stood stiffly at attention on Tuskegee Army Air Field's lone runway. The occasion was the first graduation exercise of Negro pilots into the Army Air Force. A brisk March breeze tugged at these happy cadets' dark-green officers' blouses as they stood smartly at attention before General George E. Stratemeyer, the guest speaker. A hush fell over the throng of friends and relatives as the Commanding General of the Southeastern Flying Training Command arose to speak.

"I am sure," remarked General Stratemeyer, "that everyone present, as well as the vast unseen audience of your well wishers, senses that this graduation is an historic movement, filled with portent of great good. Our country is engaged in a hard fight for its security and freedom. Here today is opened up a new source to wage that fight. It is my hope and my confident expectation that by your skill, courage, and devotion to duty you will fully justify that confidence and trust reposed in you, and that your service records will constitute bright pages in the annals of our country." Looking directly at the graduates the General continued: "You will furnish the nuclei of the 99th and 100th Pursuit Squadrons. Future graduates of this school will look up to you as 'Old Pilots.' They will be influenced profoundly by the examples which you set. Therefore, it will be of the highest importance that your service be of a character worthy of emulation by younger officers."[1]

After the address, the five new Army Air Force pilots stepped forward snappily and received their wings and commissions. Benjamin O. Davis Jr., of Washington, D. C., the son of the Army's only Negro General, Benjamin O. Davis, was the first to receive his wings. The others were Charles Debow Jr. of Indianapolis, Indiana; Lemuel R. Custis of Hartford, Connecticut; George S. Roberts of Fairmount, West Virginia; and Mac Ross of Dayton, Ohio.

The five proud young men had come a long, hard way to become members of the United States Army Air Force and at this graduation exercise they began to realize the great responsibility that rested upon them—for upon their shoulders not only rested perhaps the future of their country, but the future of Negro youths who might aspire to become pilots. These young pilots also were aware of the hardships encountered before they were admitted into the Cadet Corps.

On October 15, 1939, President Frederick D. Patterson of Tuskegee Institute was notified by Robert H. Hinckley, Chairman of the Civil Aeronautics Authority, that Tuskegee Institute had been approved for participation in the civil pilot training program. It was stipulated that Tuskegee Institute and the Alabama Air Service, a commercial flying service, would use the Municipal Airport in Montgomery, Alabama, jointly to conduct flying classes. Tuskegee Institute, however, was to conduct ground training on its campus.

In January, 1940, flight training for civil pilot trainees of Tuskegee was begun at the Municipal Airport in Montgomery with Mr. George L. Washington, Chief of Aeronautics, Tuskegee Institute as director. The daily eighty miles trip soon proved expensive and tiresome. Cognizant of this handicap, Director Washington set about to establish an air field in the vicinity of the Institute. As a result, in March, 1940, Tuskegee Institute's Airport No. 1 was opened. Meantime, while these plans were in the making, the training had progressed. In May, 1940, nineteen trainees completed flight training in the primary course and were granted private pilot certificates.

Director Washington was informed in June, 1940, by the Civil Aeronautics Authority that Tuskegee Institute had been approved for a second unit of the primary course which was to begin on June 15. A short time afterwards Dr. Patterson was notified that pilots trained at Tuskegee were eligible for two of the one thousand training scholarships being made available by the Civil Aeronautics Authority for the summer of 1940. This meant that civilian pilots trained at other colleges such as Hampton Institute, West Virginia State College, Howard University, Lincoln University, Missouri, and Lincoln University, Pennsylvania, were also eligible for two of the scholarships.

Upon receiving the information that Negro civil pilots were to be given advanced flying, President Patterson and Director Washington held a conference with high officials of the Civil Aeronautics Authority. Shortly after the conference, it was announced that advanced civil training would be held at Tuskegee Institute beginning July 22, 1940. Letters were addressed to the coordinators of civil pilot training of the various Negro colleges by Director Washington urging them to canvass their rosters of civilian pilots to secure members for the advanced course. These letters were promptly complied with and the course began as scheduled.

Although Negro youths were permitted to participate in the civilian pilot training program they were denied the right to enter military flying. In late 1940, the Air Force included in its military plan for 1941 for the establishment of ten Negro units of 250 men each, to be called Aviation Squadron (Separate). In October, 1940, the War Department announced that Negroes were in training as pilots, mechanics, and technical specialists, and that Negro Aviation Units would be organized as soon as the necessary personnel were trained. Judge William Hastie repudiated this announcement. He related that when the announcement was made the only aviation training Negroes were receiving, was training in civil flying at a few Negro colleges and one private field under the supervision of the Civil Aeronautics Administration.[2]

When it was agreed that Negroes would be accepted for military flying three principal military centers were considered as possible locations for the training of cadets. They were the West Coast, Texas, and the Southeast center of Maxwell Field in Alabama. "But Tuskegee Institute," wrote Judge Hastie, "with a small civilian pilot training program already inaugurated, was willing and anxious to cooperate with the Air Command at Maxwell Field in the development of a military aviation training program at Tuskegee to be coordinated with the Tuskegee Institute Program. In the very first step, the selection of a site for a Negro training base near Tuskegee Institute, the Administration of the school was active in the location and negotiation for the necessary land."[3]

Judge Hastie wrote in regard to the maneuver of the Administrators of the Institute: "In view of notorious racial attitudes prevalent in the Alabama and Texas areas, the integration of Negroes into the West Coast training center was the obvious course which would immediately suggest itself to anyone concerned primarily with working out a sound program."[4]

The newly proposed Tuskegee Army Air Field was to be used in the second phase of Army Aviation training. The instructors were to be military personnel. They were trained to instruct cadets who had received primary training under civilian

---

Judge William H. Hastie was Civilian Aide to the Secretary of War. On January 5, 1943, he submitted his resignation to be effective at the end of January, because of the reactionary policies and discriminatory practices of the Army Air Force in matters affecting Negroes.

instructors at privately operated schools contracted by the Army.

In organizing its primary training program the Air Force again solicited the cooperation of Tuskegee Institute. It requested the use of the facilities of the Institute for the training of cadets in the primary phase of Army flying. A contract was signed which stipulated that the Institute would furnish flying instructors, ground personnel, and the necessary physical facilities. It also provided for the stationing of a detachment of officers and enlisted men to supervise the cadet training program at the Institute's flying field. The responsibility for the operation and training in the flying school was left to the Aeronautical division of the Institute. This contract brought into being the 66th Air Force Contract Flying School at Tuskegee.

The establishment of a segregated primary school also brought protest from Judge Hastie. He wrote: "Although my own objections to a segregated Army training base were overruled in the War Department, I had persisted in contending that Negro cadets should be sent for primary training to the various contract schools, many of them outside the south where white cadets were being trained. But the plan of the Southeast center and Tuskegee Institute prevailed. Tuskegee Institute was given a contract for the primary training of all Negro cadets. The Air Command had accomplished its design for a completely segregated Negro training program."[5]

Tuskegee Institute still maintained a private civil pilot training program which had no connection with the Army training program. Many Negro youths enrolled in the civilian course with the belief that it would entitle them to further training under the Army program. Recognizing this misconception, the Institute made a request to the War Department that graduates of its civil course be given priority in admission to the Army training course. This request was readily granted by the War Department.

In spite of the apparent interest of the War Department to give Negroes military pilot training, the Air Force continued to refuse applications from Negro youths. In January, 1941, a

Howard University student, Yancey Williams, filed suit under the sponsorship of the National Association for the Advancement of Colored People to compel the Air Corps to admit him to one of the Army Air Force training centers. In early March, 1941, the Air Corps began accepting applications from Negro youths. This was followed by an announcement made by the Selective Service Headquarters on March 25, 1941. It stated, "The War Department has announced that pilots will be selected from those who have completed the secondary course offered by the Civil Aeronautics Authority. The Negro pilots, it was said, will be trained at Tuskegee, Alabama, in connection with Tuskegee Institute. Thirty-three pilots and twenty-seven planes make up the normal complement of the squadron, which was begun in February."[6]

Meantime numerous Negro youths who had been denied applications for pilot training sought aid through the National Association for the Advancement of Colored People. In a letter to Louis R. Purnell, a hopeful pilot candidate, the Association wrote on May 16, 1941:

"As one of those who have written to the N.A.A.C.P. requesting information regarding application to join the Air Corps of the United States Army, we are sending you herewith an application form. We secured these from the War Department because of the numbers of persons who had written to us, as you did.

"In making application we suggest that you request that you be given training at the training school nearest your home. Our reason for making this suggestion is because the present plan is to send such Negroes as are accepted for training to a segregated training school at Tuskegee Institute."

Signed:
Walter White
Secretary.

Shortly after the Air Corps began accepting applications from Negroes, the War Department announced that it was planning to establish an Air training center to train a Negro Squadron for pursuit flying. Following this statement by the War Department, Dr. Patterson announced that he had received a letter from the Assistant Secretary of War stating that the War Department was proceeding immediately with plans to establish a Negro Pursuit Squadron. This Squadron was to consist of 400 enlisted men, 33 pilots, and 27 planes. In addition, $1,091,000 had been appropriated for the establishment of an air field at Tuskegee.

CHAPTER II

A DREAM COMES TRUE

By the Spring of 1941 it was becoming apparent that definite plans were in the making for the acceptance of Negroes in military aviation. A new primary training school was being organized and twenty-four civilian pilots were being trained by the Army Air Force to qualify them as instructors of cadets. In the meantime, on March 21, 1941, the 99th Fighter Squadron was officially activated.

On July 10, 1941, the War Department announced that the quota of pilots for the 99th Squadron was to be about 33, but a total of approximately 100 men would be trained annually. At the same time it also stated that 271 enlisted men were already in training at Chanute Field, Illinois, as ground crews for the 99th Squadron. These men were to be sent to Tuskegee at the completion of their training and with 7 more to be entered, making a total of 278, the full ground complement would be getting technical training. The types of training these men were depicted as undergoing included airplane mechanics, aircraft armorer, aircraft supply and technical clerk, instrument and weather forecasting.

The big day for air-minded youths came on July 19, 1941. On that day an inaugural exercise marking the beginning of military pilot training for Negro youths was held at the Booker T. Washington monument, located on the campus of Tuskegee Institute. The most memorable day for the people of the little town of Tuskegee came a month later on August 25, when the first class of cadets were given their initial flying instructions.

While the first class was receiving primary training, construction of the Army Air Force Advanced Flying Field was being rushed. Early in 1941 the Army awarded a contract to

Fig. 3. THE FIRST CLASS OF NEGRO PILOTS GRADUATED AT TUSKEGEE

Fig. 4.   MECHANICS CHECK A P-40

Fig. 5.   CADETS IN TRAINING AT TUSKEGEE ARMY
AIR FIELD

McKissack and McKissack, an organization headed by a Negro architect and contractor. The contract called for the conversion of a wooded graveyard site to an airfield. On July 23, 1941, the engineers began leveling hills and uprooting trees in preparation for laying runways.

Almost at the same time the engineers began work, the Army sent Major James A. Ellison to Tuskegee to command the new field. On arriving at Tuskegee, he immediately began plans for the activation of the field. However, it was not until a month later that the real organization began.

In the latter part of October, 1941, the initial ground crew of the 99th arrived at Tuskegee Army Air Field. A few weeks later, on November 8, 1941, the first class of cadets was transferred from Primary Field to the Army Air Field and operation began.

Although Major Ellison made great progress in organizing Tuskegee Army Air Field, he was transferred on January 12, 1942, to the Air Corps Ferrying Command, Wayne County Airport in Romulus, Michigan. It was alleged that his removal was due to his courage in opposing local civil authorities who had disarmed a Negro sentry for challenging a white civilian. Major Ellison was succeeded by Colonel Frederick V. H. Kimble, a West Point graduate with twenty-four years of flying experience. It was during the period that Colonel Kimble was commanding officer that the field developed from a mere plan on paper to an actual functioning unit in the Army Air Corps. The organization of this field was not an easy one, for in addition to public sentiment which definitely affected the program, there were also flying difficulties.

When the first class completed primary training and arrived at the Advanced Flying Field, it found the field incomplete. Only one runway was sufficiently completed for flying. The ground school was located in a temporary wooden structure which housed the offices and classrooms. One of the unusual things about the building interior was that there were no partitions separating the classes from the offices. The babble of voices was accompanied by the clicking of typewriters. Concentration was most difficult for the cadets. The six cadets were divided into three classes. One could almost take lecture notes from the different classes at the same time.

Although many handicaps were present, the training went on without interruptions. In the following months more cadets were graduated as pilots and nearly every day new ground officers arrived at the field to add to the ground complement. The field was also developing rapidly. A new ground school building was constructed together with barracks, office buildings, warehouses, and a large commissary.

The organization of Tuskegee as an Air Force installation progressed so rapidly that by September, 1942, Colonel Kimble, in addressing Class 42-H, was able to remark that, though the field was still incomplete in many details, its form, utility, and purpose were well established. The following month, in addressing another class, he said that in the establishment of Tuskegee Army Air Base there appeared in the minds of those who went through its early days a far-off goal to be realized only by a long struggle of construction difficulties. As the weeks and months wore on, the goal to train pilots, to develop mechanics and to equip and organize a fighter squadron began to take tangible form and then became a concrete reality. "Today," remarked Colonel Kimble, "it is no longer difficult to see the initial goal for which you and your predecessors have stood. The Fighter Squadron exists in full fact and beyond this there are other squadrons already taking shape. The material aspects of this school are no longer difficult of realization."

Even though steady progress was made at the field, the War Department was reluctant about increasing the quota of cadets admitted for training as pilots. The order to allow only ten cadets to enter training every five weeks worked great hardship on Negro youths. Many who made applications for cadet training were delayed so long that they were called into other branches of service. Some even waited so long that they became ineligible because of the Air Corps age limit. Mr. Langston H.

Caldwell, chairman of the Tuskegee Airmen Association, in a telegram to Secretary of War Henry L. Stimson, called attention to the fact that a large number of qualified men were kept from serving their country by the ten percent restriction. "More than 100 private pilots trained at Tuskegee have filed applications to become cadets in the Air Corps, but to date only two have been called."

The National Association for the Advancement of Colored People requested that the War Department accept and train Negro cadets on the basis of fitness without regard to racial quota. The Association stated that it had received numerous letters from bewildered and disappointed young colored men who stated they had passed their physical examination but, because their actual enlistment had been delayed so long by the restricted quota system, they were being called by their local draft boards for general military service.

On December 26, 1942, Colonel Kimble was transferred to Cockron Field, Macon, Georgia to command the 27th Training Wing. He was succeeded by Colonel Noel F. Parrish. Colonel Parrish, a native of Lexington, Kentucky, was born on November 11, 1909. He obtained his elementary education in the schools of Kentucky, Georgia, and Alabama. In 1928, he was graduated from Rice Institute, Houston, Texas, with a Bachelor of Arts degree. After one year of graduate study his aspirations as a teacher gave way to a desire for travel and activity in the regular Army.

Entering the Army on July 30, 1930, as a private, Colonel Parrish spent one year with the 11th Cavalry before being appointed as a flying cadet. On the completion of his primary training at March Field, California, he was transferred with the first basic class to be trained at the newly constructed Randolph Field. Colonel Parrish completed his advance pilot training at Kelly Field in July, 1932, and was assigned to the 13th Attack Squadron then stationed at Fort Crockett, Galveston, Texas. In February, 1934, he was assigned to the First Provisional Transport Squadron. He was commissioned as a second Lieutenant in the regular Army in July, 1935, and reassigned to the 13th Attack Squadron which had moved to Barksdale Field, Louisiana. Later he was sent to Randolph Field, Texas, as a primary flight instructor.

When the civil pilot training program was inaugurated, Colonel Parrish was ordered to Chicago School of Aeronautics as an Air Corps supervisor. In May, 1941, he was sent to Tuskegee Institute to command the newly activated 66th Army Air Force Training Detachment. He and the first class of cadets to complete primary training were transferred to the Advanced Flying School at the new Tuskegee Army Air Base in November, 1941. It was at this time that he was made Director of Training.

Colonel Kimble's policy of catering to local prejudices and his determination to maintain a segregated policy on the field aroused considerable resentment. It was hoped that Colonel Parrish would change the practices at Tuskegee, but he made no substantial changes. In spite of this, Colonel Parrish's administration was more favorable than that of Colonel Kimble. Colonel Parrish was a soldier and a gentleman, with understanding and patience. He read extensively, met Negro leaders, and talked freely with everyone. As a result, he developed a keen awareness of the psychological effect of the traditional southern practices upon Negroes. This enabled him to carry out his assignment and the policy of the War Department in regard to Negroes without arousing too much resentment.

Following Colonel Parrish's elevation to the position of Commanding Officer of Tuskegee Army Air Field, the War Department broke its long silence concerning plans for Negro pilots in combat service. It announced that it expected the first Negro Squadron would very soon be on active duty overseas. It also expressed satisfaction over the results obtained in the experimental training of Negro flyers. In reference to the success of the cadets at Tuskegee, Major General James R. Ulio, Adjutant General of the Army, stated: "From results so far obtained, it is believed that the Squadron will give an excellent account of itself in combat and that it will be a credit to its race and to Americans everywhere."

Colonel Benjamin O. Davis Jr., who took over the command of the 99th Fighter Squadron on August 24, 1942, also expressed confidence in the ability of the Squadron. Speaking to an assembled group of 99th pilots and guests on the occasion of a Field Day program in December, 1942, he remarked, "The success of the combat unit will prove to be the opening wedge for the air minded youths who aspire to the field of Aviation. The records, so far, by the cadets at Tuskegee Army Flying School do not compare unfavorably with those records made by cadets at other fields. My greatest desire is to lead this squadron to victory against the enemy."

By February, 1943, it had become apparent to all at Tuskegee that definite plans were being made for the 99th to enter combat. The pilots and ground crew were given intensive training in combat tactics. Daily they were told that they must grasp as quickly as possible the various phases of training because the possibility of going into combat was great. The results of this intensive training program were evident by the remark made by Secretary of War Stimson on his visit to Tuskegee in February, 1943, when he stated that the outfit looked as good as any he had seen.

It was shortly after Secretary Stimson's visit that the possibility of active overseas duty seemed to become a probability. Colonel Parrish, addressing the 99th Fighter Squadron on February 12, hinted as much when he stated: "All of you know that any time you may be sent into an active combat zone. Since none of us can foretell the day of your departure from the station and the command, I shall take this occasion to speak a few words of farewell.

"You are fighting men now. You have made the team. Your future is now being handed into your own hands. No one knows what you will do with your future as fighting men, you yourselves do not know. Your future, good or bad, will depend largely on how determined you are not to give satisfaction to those who would like to see you fail."

Throughout the month of March, 1943, the 99th Squadron went through intensive and rigorous training. The pilots were not only drilled in the fundamentals of aerial combat, formation flying, and night flying but, with the ground complement, were subjected to long forced marches and drilled in bivouac and Air Base maintenance procedures.

Finally, on the morning of April 1, 1943, the 99th began making preparation for its departure from Tuskegee. Although the movement of the Squadron was supposed to be kept as confidential as possible, the news of its leaving for combat spread throughout the little town of Tuskegee. The next day, April 2, hundreds of well wishers and friends gathered at the depot to bid the men farewell and good luck as they boarded the evacuation train.

CHAPTER III

THE ROAD TO WAR

Although the members of the 99th had suspicion that they were headed for overseas duty, they were not convinced until they arrived at Camp Shanks, New York, a port of embarkation. Upon arrival, they were given quarters, fed, and for the remainder of the day they were allowed to lounge around and rest. The next morning the long tedious job of being processed began. This lasted for ten days. Finally, on the morning of April 14, Colonel Davis, who was to be senior officer aboard the transport ship, was directed to select a staff consisting of an Adjutant, Mess Officer, Provost Marshal, and Police Officer to aid him as Executive Officer in carrying out the orders and policies of the Transport Commander. It was now obvious that their stay in the country was to be only a matter of days.

The order to board ship came sooner than many expected. Early next morning, April 15, the Squadron was ordered to board ship. This was it! Although everyone saw it coming, the news was still a surprise. For a moment there was almost a complete silence—then confusion reigned. All of the men began talking simultaneously—talking of seeing their kids once more, of their wives and loved ones, of being back on "Main Street," of their chances for survival, of the war in general.

A few hours later, the transport, filled to capacity with approximately four thousand troops, white and colored, officers and enlisted men, hoisted anchor and stole out of the harbor. It was still dark and seemingly more quiet than usual as the ship moved lazily down the Hudson towards the sea. Its deck was crowded to capacity with men trying to get their last look at their native land.

[25]

The ship was far out at sea when the sun rose. The men could still see the majestic skyscrapers towering in the sky. Sadness filled their hearts as they watched the last vestige of their country slowly disappear in the hazy distance.

The first day at sea many of the men suffered from sea sickness. But as the days passed they became more accustomed to the water. They moved about more at ease, played games, and met members of other squadrons. Still they could not completely relax for they lived in anticipation of attacks by enemy U-boats.

For eight days the ship moved steadily ahead. On the morning of April 24, land was sighted. There was a mad rush for the deck, for every porthole, for every window. Land! Land! was the cry on every lip. As the minutes and the hours passed by slowly, the men became restless. Everyone now was excited and curious. It seemed as if they would never reach shore.

Finally, in the late afternoon, the ship entered the harbor and shortly afterwards dropped anchor. The wharves were crowded with Arabs who begged candies and cigarettes and fought among themselves over the prizes tossed from the ships by the soldiers.

The job of disembarkation was long and tedious. After casting anchor the ship stood at dock for hours before the first troop disembarked. When the movement finally began only one outfit at a time was permitted to leave the ship. It was hot and the waiting seemed endless to the men who were now almost exhausted from the heat and the long voyage.

When the 99th's turn came to disembark the men hurried down the gang-plank. As they reached the ground they were besieged by a host of Arabs who swarmed around them and begged for cigarettes and food.

The squadron was met by Colonel Allison of the Northwest Training Command. After greeting Colonel Davis, he directed the movement of the squadron to its bivouac area.

En route to the new station the convoy passed through the

city of Casablanca. The men observed the white buildings and green squares. They saw Moroccans in their bright red uniforms; they viewed French Colonials sitting at the tables of sidewalk cafés and noticed Arabs in turbans, sandals, and dirty white robes milling about the streets.

It was late afternoon when the convoy reached the bivouac area. Although tired and hungry, the men set about in good spirit to set up camp. Colonel Davis meanwhile was busy seeking information relative to his new station.

When the sun went down the temperature dropped considerably. By now the men were almost exhausted, so after a hearty meal they turned in for a good night's rest.

The following day Colonel Davis and his operations officer, Captain George S. Roberts, were taken by Colonel Allison to see General Camp, who commanded the Northwest Training Command. General Camp persuaded Colonel Davis to remain in the area until the squadron was satisfactorily equipped for combat. He also sent Colonel Davis on a preliminary reconnaissance of his new station, which was located about one hundred and fifty miles inland in French Morocco near the town of Fez in North Africa.

After the 99th Squadron was equipped to the satisfaction of Colonel Davis, arrangements were made to move by rail to the new station. It was a slow, tiresome ride, and to these men who had come across the sea with expectations of finding everyone rushing with excitement this was a great disappointment.

It took the train seventeen hours to cover the 150 miles. During the trip Colonel Davis complained about the slowness of the train. He was informed that he was lucky to move at such a fast rate of speed.

Upon arrival at the new station, which was located at OuedN'ja, a little town near Fez, the 99th immediately began setting up camp. Knowing that they would be stationed here for a while, the men set about to make their quarters as comfortable as possible.

A service command was stationed near the 99th's new location. It was commanded by a Colonel Phillips. A fighter-bomber group was also located nearby. It was commanded by Colonel Stevenson, a West Point graduate whom Colonel Davis had met at the Academy. Colonel Davis, relating the experiences at OuedN'ja said: "Our stay there was probably our most pleasant stay overseas. Most cordial relations existed between the members of the Squadron and the members of the fighter-bomber group nearby. The pilots of the two organizations engaged in impromptu dog fights to determine the relative superiority of the P-40 and the A-36. Enlisted men of the two groups got along together very well in all types of athletic contest and other means of recreation.

"The town of Fez was found to be one of the most delightful spots that any of us had ever visited. One unusual feature of our stay there was that members of my organization and members of these organizations visited the town of Fez every single night for over a period of a month, and not one unpleasant incident arose.

"The officers of the squadron were made socially secure in the town by the visit of Josephine Baker. Miss Baker insisted on presenting several different groups of our officers to the prominent French and Arab families in the town. All in all Miss Baker was very largely responsible for our most pleasant social relations in the town of Fez.

"It was during our stay here that four P-39 pilots, whom we had met on the boat on the way over, came to visit us. They were ferrying some P-39s from Oran to Casablanca and en route they, of their own volition, simply stopped over to pay us a visit. I mention this simply to indicate that a considerable bond existed among those who fly regardless of color or race.

"Our equipment was of the best. We ferried in twenty-seven brand new P-40s and all of us experienced for the first time the thrill of flying a brand new airplane. Lieutenant Colonel Phillip Cockron—the Flip Corkin of 'Terry and the Pirates' —was our most capable instructor. He imbued all of us with some of his own very remarkable fighting spirit, and in addition to that he taught us what to do and what not to do in aerial combat.

"We had two other instructors who were with us until we left for Tunisia, Major Keyes and a Captain Fachler. Both of these officers had extensive combat training, one in England and one in the African campaign, and both had just been returned to the training command for instructional purposes. These officers worked unceasingly to make us ready for the real test and all of us felt very grateful for their efforts."[1]

CHAPTER IV

A TASTE OF COMBAT

The members of the 99th soon learned that war was not as static as it appeared. After spending a month of intensive combat training at OuedN'ja, the Squadron was ordered to move to a new base on the Cape Bon Peninsula.

On May 31, 1943, the air echelon of the 99th flew to its new station at Fardjouna in North Africa where it entered its final phase of training. Upon arrival at Fardjouna, the 99th was attached to the 33rd Fighter Group, which was commanded by Colonel William Monyer.

It was now evident to the pilots of the 99th that they were gradually being integrated into the great fighting machine that was taking the battle to the enemy. At this station they received first hand information from pilots who were daily meeting the enemy. They saw planes return to the base riddled with holes from enemy machine gun fire. They saw planes hobble home almost torn apart. They waited for friends who never returned. They saw pilots die. These things brought the war home to the members of the 99th. Now they realized that they had no time to waste—that their futures were left up to themselves.

The first combat assignment of the 99th came on June 2, 1943. The mission was a strafing mission against the heavily fortified island of Pantelleria. In reference to the Squadron's entrance into combat, Colonel Davis said: "I personally believe that no unit in this war had gone into combat better trained or better equipped than the 99th Fighter Squadron. We were weak in one respect only and that was simply that the Squadron Commander, myself, and the flight commanders had had no actual combat experience. That is a very desirable feature because it gives a bit of confidence to those who are led that the man who is in charge of the formation knows what he is doing, and frankly, I didn't know initially, nor did my flight commanders. On the other hand, this deficiency was balanced by the fact that my pilots averaged about 250 hours in a P-40, and a young pilot in these days who has 250 hours in a P-40 before he goes into combat is a hard man to find."

Colonel Davis assigned four men for his pioneering role. The pilots assigned to make the first combat missions were Lieuts. Charles B. Hall, William A. Campbell, Clarence C. Jamison and James T. Wiley. Another pilot, Lemuel R. Custis, was also chosen to be one of the pioneers, but at the time had not arrived at the base because his plane had developed engine trouble en route from OuedN'ja. All of these men were to fly as wingmen for pilots of the 33rd Fighter Group.

The morning of June 2 was one of the most important days for the squadron, for it was on this morning that Lieuts. Hall and Campbell received the necessary briefing for the first combat mission. After the briefing, Hall and Campbell were taken to the dispersal area in a jeep. On arrival at the area, they jumped out of the jeep and walked swiftly towards their planes. When they reached their planes they climbed in and, with the aid of their crew chiefs, adjusted their equipment. This completed, the crew chiefs stepped down off the wings of the planes. The two pilots then started the engines and taxied up the runway for the take off. Hall led and Campbell followed closely behind. As they reached the edge of the runway they stopped their planes and raced their engines. The roar of the two planes sounded unusually loud, but, to the jubilant members of the squadron, who had assembled to watch the take off, there was undescribable beauty in this roar.

When the planes were sufficiently warmed Hall and Campbell started off. After traveling a short distance, they gunned their planes and rose swiftly into the air. The crowd kept its eyes on the two planes until they disappeared into the distance.

At eight o'clock when Lieuts. Jamison and Wiley left on the squadron's second mission the squadron witnessed another spectacle. Later in the afternoon the same pilots made another flight to Pantelleria, but no enemy aircraft was sighted that day, and on the whole the initial missions were unexciting.

The 99th flew missions to Pantelleria for seven days without sighting the first enemy aircraft. Finally, on the morning of June 9, a flight led by Lieut. Charles Dryden of New York City was attacked by a group of enemy aircraft.

Just before reaching his rendezvous point, Dryden heard a call over his radio, "Unidentified aircraft approaching the island." Immediately Dryden reefed his plane around with his flight following him. Behind him were Lieuts. Lee Rayford of Ardwick, Maryland; Willie Ashley of Sumter, South Carolina; Spann Watson of Hackensack, New Jersey; Sidney P. Brooks of Cleveland, Ohio; and Leon Roberts of Pritchard, Alabama.

Training a pilot is a long process. Flying an airplane is only a part of that process. The rest has to be gained through experience. The fighter pilot gains the greater portion of his knowledge from his fellow pilots and from the enemy. There are two things a fighter pilot must have to be successful in combat: confidence in his ability to kill, and confidence in his ability to get away when in trouble. These can only be acquired through active participation in combat. If the pilot feels he can kill and feels that the enemy can't kill him, then he has the offensive spirit. Without that offensive spirit—the ability to attack instantaneously and automatically like a tiger the moment he spots an enemy plane—he is lost. If he hangs back and is afraid to take the offensive, he eventually gets shot down.

Realizing that they would probably be attacked, the pilots settled tight against their seats and tensed a little against the pull of their planes' engines. They were nervous, of course, because this was to be their first encounter with the enemy who had been credited as shrewd and capable pilots. But though they lacked the confidence in their ability to shoot down the enemy and figured they didn't know enough about the business of fighting with planes to match the enemy skill, they realized that they had to fight to survive.

As they climbed to gain altitude for an attack, the enemy planes dodged in over the sea. Suddenly Lieut. Roberts spied the enemy flight as it dived out of the sun. Lieut. Roberts broke to the right to evade the enemy aircraft that were now coming down on his formation at great speed. As he broke, the rest of the flight broke with him. But, though previously warned by the air observer, they had been caught by surprise. It was impossible for them to maintain company front against the Germans who were diving in loose formation of two's at approximately 450 miles an hour.

Lieut. Dryden after turning found himself far out beyond the enemy aircraft, with the bombers passing about 5000 feet above. He pointed the nose of his plane upward and began climbing towards the bombers. After climbing far above the enemy formation, he circled and fell into a dive. He dived at full speed across the tail end of the enemy formation and sprayed the enemy ships with a few volleys of 50 caliber fire as he went along. On pulling up, he noticed a dog fight. Without hesitation, he went to the aid of his comrades who were battling desperately to match the skilled and experienced Germans.

In the meantime Lieut. Lee Rayford was having trouble with two Focke Wulfs which had caught him alone. They kept charging at his plane and each time he attacked one, the other would attack. Although this was Rayford's first engagement, he kept his composure and fought back with great determination. A 20 millimeter cannon shell shattered his right wing, but he fought back. He had been taught that the best defensive against the enemy was a determined offensive, and in battle the lesson stuck with him. The Germans pressed the battle with equal determination. They attacked from all angles and maneuvered to line him up for the kill. Just when it seemed that they would be successful, Lieut. Spann Watson came to the rescue of Rayford. Watson opened up at long range on one of the attacking planes and to his surprise hit his target. The Germans, seeing that opposition was gathering against them, retreated.

At the initial turn, Lieut. Willie Ashley's plane had gone into a spin, causing him to lose considerable altitude. When he came out of the spin, he saw another plane out alone. Thinking it was a friendly plane, he decided to join the aircraft, but as he closed in on the plane, he found it to be a Focke-Wulf. He moved in closer and began to fire. He sprayed the enemy aircraft with several volleys before it began to smoke and headed downward. Ashley dived after the smoking plane, but as he approached the ground the enemy ground force sent up a heavy barrage of flak and machine gun fire. Ashley was forced to turn back, and as a result probably lost the opportunity of being the first Negro to destroy an enemy aircraft in aerial combat.

This air assault on Pantelleria which began on May 30, 1943, caused the Italian island of 11,500 population to surrender on June 11. Thus, for the first time in history, air power alone had completely destroyed all enemy resistance.

On June 12, Lampedusa, another island, succumbed to the allied air attack, and the following day Limosa, a third island, surrendered. The capture of these islands gave allied sea power complete control of the sea lanes to Sicily and Italy.

Fig. 6.   SECRETARY OF WAR STIMSON INSPECTS
THE 99TH SQUADRON

Fig. 7.   BRIGADIER GENERAL BENJAMIN O. DAVIS
VISITS TUSKEGEE

left, General Davis—center, Lt. Col. Noel F. Parrish—
right, Lt. Col. B. O. Davis, Jr.

Fig. 8. MEMBERS OF THE ORIGINAL 99TH FIGHTER SQUADRON

CHAPTER V

THE SICILIAN CAMPAIGN

After the fall of Pantelleria, the Allies turned their attention to the island of Sicily. By capturing Sicily, they believed that allied troops would be in a position to successfully invade Italy. However, the immediate objective of the Allies was to capture Messina, an enemy port in northeastern Sicily. Through this port almost all enemy supplies flowed, and once it was secured the position of the enemy in Sicily would be hopeless.

On June 29 the 99th Fighter Squadron moved to El Haouria on the tip of Cape Bon. Here it began operating with the 324th Fighter Group which was engaged in the battle of Sicily.

The 99th's first mission to the island was on July 1, 1943, when it was assigned to escort medium bombers to the western sector of Sicily. Although the mission was successful, it was unexciting, for the pilots encountered very little enemy opposition.

The next day, July 2, the 99th was assigned to escort medium bombers to the coast of Sicily in the Castelvetrano area. The pilots who were to make the flight reported at the briefing room after an early breakfast. The Intelligence Officer began the briefing immediately. He revealed the target, the amount and position of enemy anti-aircraft batteries, and the number of enemy fighters expected to be encountered in the target area. When the Intelligence Officer finished, the Weather Officer gave the weather report. The pilots were then told to synchronize their watches. The briefing was over.

After leaving the briefing room, the pilots rode to the dispersal area where the planes had already been warmed up and were ready for the take off. A few minutes later, the first plane broke ground. Others followed at short intervals. As they climbed they circled the base until the flight was assembled. Then the flight headed towards the coast and picked up the bombers.

The sky was clear although there was a slight ground haze. Only a few minutes had elapsed before they were over the Mediterranean, which was calm, clear, and remarkably blue.

Once clear of the land, the pilots tested their guns. As they engaged their triggers the sharp rat-a-tat-tat of the practice shells sang out above the noise of the engines. Satisfied that their guns were in firing condition, the pilots fell into position to cover the bombers.

On arriving in the target area, the bombers began to unload their bombs. Clouds of smoke arose from the explosions. This was answered by volleys of inaccurate, large, black flak bursts. Almost immediately a group of enemy fighters came up to attack the bombers.

When the enemy planes were sighted the 99th broke formation and charged them. In the ensuing battle, the 99th received its first aerial victory when Lieut. Charles B. Hall of Brazil, Indiana, shot down a Focke Wulf 190. Relating his victory, Hall said: "It was my eighth mission and the first time I had seen the enemy close enough to shoot at him. I saw two Focke-Wulfs following the bombers just after the bombs were dropped. I headed for the space between the fighters and bombers and managed to turn inside the Jerries. I fired a long burst and saw my tracers penetrate the second aircraft. He was turning to the left, but suddenly fell off and headed straight into the ground. I followed him down and saw him crash. He raised a big cloud of dust."

At the time Hall was gaining the Squadron's first victory, Lieut. Charles Dryden and his wingman Lieut. James B. Knighten were fighting a grim battle against four German aircraft. When the formation broke to attack the enemy planes, Dryden noticed two Messerschmidt 109s making passes at the outside bomber element. After the enemy attacked the bombers, they pulled up and began to split "S." Dryden, who was above the attacking enemy aircraft, made a dive for the enemy as his wingman followed. He was about to fire on one of the enemy ships when two Focke-Wulfs opened up on him. He was forced to break off his attack and go into a series of tight turns to avoid being shot down.

The Germans were determined to make the kill. They pressed the attack and maneuvered to line up the fleeing planes. But, after following the attack for a long while and seeing that they were being led too far from their base, the Germans broke off the attack. When Dryden landed at the base, he found his ship had been severely damaged.

The success of Lieut. Hall was received with praise by the Allied Commanders. General Dwight D. Eisenhower made a special visit to the base and upon arrival exclaimed, "I would like to meet the pilot who shot down the Jerry." Among General Eisenhower's party were General Carl Spaatz, Major General Doolittle, and Air Marshal Cunningham of the Royal Air Force.

Amid the joy and celebration of Lieut. Hall's victory there was also sadness. A few hours earlier, Lieut Sherman White Jr. of Montgomery, Alabama, and Lieut. James L. McCullin of St. Louis, Missouri, collided while taking off on an early morning mission. Both pilots were killed.

Throughout the first week of July, 1943, the 99th continued its attacks on the island of Sicily. It escorted medium bombers to bomb the coastal batteries and enemy installations. It strafed enemy air fields and dive bombed supply centers and communication lines.

These relentless attacks played a potent part in a softening up of the island for the invasion of the ground forces. On July 7, the invasion fleet slipped out of the harbor of North Africa and headed for Sicily. Ernie Pyle, one the United States' most outstanding War Correspondents, vividly described the invasion of Sicily.

"Our first day at sea was like a peacetime Mediterranean

cruise. The weather was something you read about in travel folders, gently warm and sunny and the sea as smooth as velvet.[1] On the second day, the dawn came up gray and misty with a forty mile an hour gale. The sea was rough and all day long the invasion troops were harassed by the continuous rocking, bouncing, and swaying of the ship. At ten o'clock I lay down with my clothes on. There wasn't anything I could do and the rolling sea was beginning to take nibbles at my stomach, too. As I finally fell asleep the wind was still howling and the ship was pounding and falling through space.

"The next thing I knew a booming voice over the ship's loudspeaker was saying, 'Stand by for gunfire. We may have to shoot out some searchlights.'

"I jumped up, startled. The engines were stopped. There seemed to be no wind. The entire ship was motionless and quiet as a grave. I grabbed my helmet, ran out on the deck, and stared over the rail. We were anchored, and we could see the dark shapes of the Sicilian hills not far away. The water lapped with gentle caressing sound against the sides of the ship. We had arrived. The storm was gone. I looked down and the surface of the Mediterranean was slick and smooth as a table top. Already assault boats were skimming past us towards the shore. Not a breath of air stirred. The miracle had happened."[2]

It was approximately 2:45 A.M., July 10, when the first wave of troops stormed the beaches. As they waded in, the guns from the naval vessels kept up a continuous barrage of fire. They were answered by the enemy batteries which were located on the hills back of the beaches. Throughout the early morning the battle raged. Finally the enemy fire began to dwindle, and the superiority of the Allied force became evident.

Daybreak found the shores of Sicily clustered with assault boats and the American Flag flying majestically above an enemy fort. The Allies had landed safely and established the beachhead as planned.

In the meantime the 99th Fighter Squadron was doing its part in making the invasion a success. While the invasion fleet was at sea, the 99th Fighter Squadron guarded the fleet against being attacked by enemy planes. It made numerous divebombing and strafing missions and escorted medium bombers to the island.

On the afternoon of July 10, Lieut. Richard Bolling of Hampton, Virginia, was shot down while patrolling the invasion area. His plane was severely damaged by flak and started to burn. Bolling bailed out of his burning ship and landed in the Mediterranean Sea. Lieut. Samuel Bruce of Seattle, Washington, circled Bolling and pin-pointed his position before returning to the base.

After spending twenty-four hours drifting helplessly, Bolling was picked up by an American destroyer and set ashore in Sicily. Several days later he boarded a ship for North Africa and returned to the base. Meantime, on July 10, the 99th completed its operations with the 324th and prepared to move to a new base in Sicily. In the eleven days of operations with the 324th, it flew 175 sorties, divebombing and strafing enemy positions.

By this time the American Seventh Army had swung west and north from Licata and Gela to mop up the western half of the island, while the British Eighth Army under General Montgomery advanced up the east coast from Noto and Syracuse towards Messina. The strategy was to trap the enemy in the Northeastern corner of Sicily to prevent the enemy escape across the Strait of Messina to Italy.

On July 14, the Americans captured the Biscari airfield which assured them a good base for aerial operation against the enemy. On July 19, the 99th moved to Licata, Sicily, a city of 35,000 inhabitants, located on the coast of the Mediterranean Sea.

On July 23, the 99th received its first group of replacement pilots. They were: Lieuts. Howard Baugh of Petersburg, Virginia; Edward L. Toppins of San Francisco, California; John Morgan of Carterville, Georgia; John Gibson of Chicago, Illinois; and Herman A. Lawson of Maryville, California.

Meantime, on July 22, the coastal city of Agrigento was captured, and a week later Palermo fell to the swiftly advancing Americans. The Allied troops advanced so rapidly that the Axis forces began preparing to withdraw across the Strait of Messina. A race began for the Strait, with the British pushing up from the South and the Americans driving in from the North.

The 99th was still in operation against the enemy. It dive bombed strongholds, strafed enemy troops, patrolled the areas, and performed armed reconnaissance. On August 11, Lieut. Paul Mitchell of Washington, D. C. was killed when his plane crashed into a plane piloted by Lieut. Samuel Bruce of Seattle, Washington. Fortunately, Lieut. Bruce escaped death by parachuting to safety.

In spite of the all-out drive by the Allied Ground Forces, the 12th Air Force, and a series of amphibious landings, the Germans were able to retreat across the Strait of Messina. On August 17, 1943, the U. S. 3rd Division pushed into the town of Messina. A little later, a detachment from the Eighth Army arrived in Messina. The remaining element of the enemy forces was soon eliminated. It had taken just 38 days to capture the Island and approximately 100,000 prisoners.

CHAPTER VI

THE DARK DAYS

Preparations for the invasion of Italy were made immediately after the conquest of Sicily. The Allied strategy called for landing troops at Salerno, to speed the conquest of Italy and to secure airfields for continued attacks upon strategic enemy targets. Its initial landing objective was to establish a beachhead twenty-five miles inland and twelve miles deep in the Salerno area and make contact with the British 8th Army moving from the South.

The first invasion movement began on September 3, 1943, when General Montgomery slipped two divisions of the famous British Eighth Army across from Messina to Reggio Calabria and advanced up the Italian coast against slight resistance. This was followed by an invasion in the Salerno area on September 8, by American forces. The following day, on September 9, a third invasion of Italy took place when the British First Airborne Division captured the Taranto Naval Base, which was located in Taranto Harbor.

In an attempt to halt the American drive in the Salerno area, the enemy withdrew large numbers of troops who were resisting General Montgomery's advance. On September 11, the Germans counterattacked on the Salerno front and recaptured valuable territories between the Sele and Calore rivers. The enemy could not follow up its victories, however, and by September 15 was forced to withdraw to the North.

The retreating Germans were pursued by the American Fifth and British Eighth Armies which had joined south of Salerno Bay on September 13. While the Salerno forces were driving the Germans northward, the British First Airborne

Division was pushing its way to Foggia. The capture of Foggia gave the Allies access to valuable air bases.

The fall of Sicily spurred the Allied Mediterranean Air Force into action against the Italian Peninsula. Fighter planes, medium bombers, and heavy bombers ranged the whole length of the peninsula to soften up the enemy for the assault by the ground forces. They ruined air fields, pinned enemy aircraft on the ground, destroyed enemy planes that rose to intercept them, and struck communication lines around and far beyond the invasion area. During the invasion, the Air Force covered the invasion troops and supported the ground troops as they advanced inland.

This assignment of divebombing gave the pilots little opportunity to engage enemy aircraft. On September 11, 1943, the 99th was moved to a base in Italy and was given the assignment of divebombing and strafing. Throughout the Sicilian and Salerno campaigns the 99th Squadron flew numerous missions without sighting enemy aircraft. Meanwhile, on September 18, 1943, the Squadron lost one of its pilots. Lieut. Sidney Brooks of Cleveland, Ohio, was killed while taking off on a dive bombing mission.

When Colonel George Spencer Roberts returned to the States in the early part of 1944, he spoke as guest speaker at a ceremony held at the Abraham Lincoln Garden located at East Boulevard and Wade Park Avenue, Cleveland, Ohio. The occasion was the planting of an evergreen tree as a memorial for Lieut. Brooks. During the course of the speech Colonel Roberts remarked:

"Sidney Brooks fought and stood for the things that are America. America is its people—you. We are finding that the color of a man's skin, the blood in his veins, or his religion makes no difference in finding whether he is or is not a man. The privileges of America belong to those brave and strong enough to fight for them."

Mayor Frank J. Lausche spoke of the death of a young man who gave everything in defense of a democracy he did not enjoy, in the hope that his death might make it possible for the living to continue to fight for an America that would be free, just and fair for all people.

The failure of the 99th to gain aerial victories caused some high army officials to suspect its pilots' courage to fight. They charged the 99th with being a failure and clamored for more action. However, while the 99th was being criticized, Lieut. Colonel Phillip C. Cockron, one of the United States Army's greatest dive bombing experts, was praising the 99th as "a collection of born dive bombers."

Although the 99th was criticized for failing to register aerial victories on dive bombing and strafing missions, seemingly the records of other dive bombing units were not taken into consideration. For instance, Ernie Pyle, who covered the Mediterranean theatre of war during the Sicilian and Italian campaigns, wrote: "For several reasons our dive bombers didn't have much trouble with German fighters. First of all, the Luftwaffe was weak over there at the time. Then, too, the dive bombers' job was to work on the infantry front lines, so they seldom got back to where the German fighters were. Also the invader itself was such a good fighter that the Jerries weren't too anxious to tangle with it.

"There were pilots in the squadron who had finished their allotted missions and gone back to America without ever firing a shot at an enemy plane in the air. And that's the way it should be, for their job was to dive bomb, not to get caught in a fight."[1]

The pilots of other outfits also experienced the lack of air opposition during the Sicilian and Salerno campaigns. Lieut. William Murphy, a P-38 pilot whose group covered the assault troops over Salerno, related: "We left after dawn and picked up warships, transports, and landing craft just off Salerno. I could see the activity beneath us and it appeared that there was not much in the way of opposition. We assumed our position over the beachhead in groups of four in stepped down strings. Throughout the first day, we didn't have any aerial opposition. We just went up and back, up and back, without any trouble.

There were control boats in the water to warn us of approaching planes, but during the first day there just wasn't anything to warn us about."[2]

The same was true for the top cover spitfires—no German aerial activity—according to Captain Dale E. Shafer. "I was over the invasion area with the first element," he recalled, "and it was just like a practice mission. All we did was fly around for a while and then go back to our base while another group took over."[3]

Colonel Fred M. Dean, writing of his experiences in the Sicilian campaign, related: "There was scarcely any contest in the sky over Sicily. The few fighters we met seemed more interested in turning tail and evading combat than in attempting to press interference with our invasion operations. The transports and bombers encountered likewise were easy pickings. Enemy air activity was relatively negligible and in a way we were surprised with the lack of opposition."[4]

The protest against the 99th combat record reached national attention on September 20, 1943, when *Time Magazine* carried an article on the "99th Fighter Squadron." The article stated that the 99th had made such a poor demonstration overseas that it was being considered by the War Department to disband the organization as a fighter unit.[5]

Almost immediately after the article appeared in *Time*, Colonel Davis, who had been recalled to the States on September 2, held a press conference at the War Department. In relating the attitude of his squadron Colonel Davis said that the members of the 99th realized that the unit was a test to determine whether the Negro pilot was physically, mentally, and emotionally suited to the rigors of combat flying. They understood that the future of the Negro in the Air Corps probably would be largely dependent upon the manner in which they carried out their mission. Hence, the importance of the work done by the squadron meant that very little pleasure was to be had by anyone until the experiment was deemed an unqualified success. He added that the outfit was hurt by the adverse public-

[44]

ity it received during the training period at Tuskegee. The men, however, had the sense to realize that the best means they had to defeat the ends of supporters and philosophers who relegated them to a subsidiary role in the life of the United States was to do their job in such a way that the world would know that they were capable of performing a highly specialized and technical piece of work in a creditable manner.

Lieut. Colonel George S. Roberts, who also commanded the 99th Fighter Squadron, said: "People assumed the 99th was not producing because they were Negroes. It was remarkable that the men kept their morale, being under such a strain because of the civilian attitude. We went for months without seeing an enemy aircraft, not to mention shooting at one."

The War Department repudiated the story that it was contemplating the deactivation of the 99th Squadron. It stated that it "felt keenly about the report" which appeared in *Time*. An Air Force officer stated that the Office of the Assistant Chief of Air Staff, Operations, Commitments and Requirements had no knowledge of such a proposal; and that so little operational data on the 99th had reached Washington that it was impossible to form a conclusive opinion about the pilots. He added that the 99th had apparently seen little action compared with many other units, but seemed to have done fairly well.

However, unofficial reports from the Mediterranean theatre had suggested that the top air command was not altogether satisfied with the 99th's performance.[5] Although the War Department denied it had considered disbanding the 99th, it was no secret to Colonel Davis and his staff that General Arnold, the wartime Chief of the Army Air Force, had listened to the unofficial and prejudiced reports and had considered the disbandment of the Squadron. Lieut Colonel George S. Roberts in relating a visit of General Arnold to the base said, "I never felt so bad in all my life. While he stood there discrediting the men who were doing their best under the circumstances, I felt like crying. I could see that Colonel Davis also was deeply hurt."

CHAPTER VII

FROM FAILURE TO SUCCESS

The capture of Salerno was a strategic gain for the Allies. They were now in a position to take the offensive against the enemy forces stationed in Italy. The Germans began to withdraw to the North followed by both the Fifth and Eighth Armies. On September 23, 1943, Oliveto was captured by the British Eighth Army. The Germans then fell back to defend Naples. On October 7, the Fifth Army, with the aid of uprising civilians, forced the Germans to surrender the city of Naples and fall back to the steep northern bank of the Volturno river.

There was no rest for the Germans. On October 9, 1943, the 79th Fighter Group moved to Foggia and shortly afterwards was joined by the 99th Fighter Squadron. The 99th went into action with the 79th Group by attacking targets in the Isernia—Capinone area and later shifted to the network of roads northwest of Sangro. Meantime, on October 16, the enemy was forced to retreat from its position on the Volturno. However, in its retreat, the Germans destroyed bridges, and left land mines and small groups of snipers that forced the Allies to move with caution. The muddy season had also set in, making the task of following the retreating enemy all the more difficult. Herbert L. Mathews, a noted War Corespondent, wrote of the mud of Italy, "No mud could be deeper or stickier or more persistent. On flat ground you plow disgustedly through it, often getting into it well over your ankles. But on a climb you do worse. You slide, slip, fall all over yourself and get covered with it from your head to feet. The more tired you get the more you slip and fall, the dirtier you get the harder it is to stand up again and plug on."[1]

Progress was slow on all fronts, but the Allies continued

their relentless attacks. On November 19, the 99th moved with the 79th Fighter Group to Madna, a coastal strip near Termoli. But the bad weather continued to limit flying. Clear weather on November 30 permitted the 79th Group to set a record by flying twenty-six missions. The Group also had good weather on Dec. 1. In the two days of flying it dropped sixty-five tons of bombs on the heavily defended area around Orsogna. In one day, the 99th Squadron flew nine missions and the 87th Fighter Squadron flew eight. This included loading bombs, cleaning guns, refueling and repairing. Damaged aircraft were repaired, props were changed, and instruments adjusted practically on the spot. Not only were the crew chiefs kept continuously busy, but the armorers, fitters, and mechanics worked right up to the last minute. These missions enabled the 8th Army to establish a beachhead across the Sangro and won for the 79th Fighter Group many congratulatory messages.

The 79th Fighter Group with the 99th fighting as a component, averaged thirty-six to forty-eight sorties a day, striking close support targets on the lateral roads branching out of Chieti. After dropping their bombs the pilots strafed troop concentrations, gun positions, and convoys. Intense small arms fire supplemented by heavy and light anti-aircraft fire and extremely bad weather made the mission very hazardous, but the pilots refused to quit.

A series of close support targets was communicated to the 79th Group by the Air Support Control of the 8th Army. These targets extended from Ortona to Orsogna and as far west as Chieti. They were important because they meant defended positions, mortars, big guns, or troop concentrations which stood in the way of General Montgomery's advance up the east coast. On the missions many pilots suffered ack-ack hits before their dive bombing attacks, but chose to complete their assignments.

The bravery of the pilots in carrying out their missions brought numerous commendations to the 79th Group, both from the British and Dominion Commanders of the 8th Army.

It was related that the air attacks caused countless German casualties, destroyed vast amounts of enemy equipment and buildings, and forced the Germans to make hasty withdrawals. This enabled Allied troops to enter the areas without too much resistance from the disorganized enemy forces.

On December 18, 1943, an all out air assault in support of New Zealand and Indian Divisions thrusting towards Orsogna and Tollo was called. Thirty missions were flown by the 57th and 79th Groups, the RAF 239th Wing and SAAF spitbombers of Squadron No. 4 against enemy gun positions and installations. However, bad weather hid many of the targets. In spite of the indifferent weather, by noon of the 18th, fourteen missions had successfully bombed their targets. Nine missions brought back their bombs, while four bombed alternate targets discovered through the gaps in the clouds.

Meantime, early in December General Clark's Fifth Army cleared the Germans out of the Camino hills. It then consolidated its position for a drive on the winter line in mid January. In an effort to break the winter stalemate, the Allies planned an end around assault at Anzio.

On January 15, 1944, the 99th moved with the 79th Group from Madna to the Capidachino Airdrome near Naples. Here it began operation on January 18, protecting Allied vessels shelling enemy strongholds from the Gulf of Gaeta, north of Naples. On January 22, 1944, three divisions of Allied troops landed at Nettuno and Anzio while the Allied Air Force struck at targets around the beachhead and in Southern France.

The Germans, preoccupied at Cassino, were taken by surprise and the quick Allied drive moved within Aprilia before gathering German resistance stopped its advance. Here three Axis Divisions, including Italian Fascista, still held the heights commanding the beachhead. Ernie Pyle wrote of the battle that followed at Anzio:

"On the beachhead every inch of our territory was under German Artillery fire. There was no rear area that was immune, as in most battle zones. They could reach us with their 88's and they used everything from that on up . . . The land of the Anzio beachhead is flat and our soldiers felt strange and naked with no rocks to take cover behind, no mountains to provide slopes for protection. It was a new kind of warfare for us. Distances were short and space was confined. The whole beachhead was the front line, so small that we could stand on high ground in the middle of it and see clear around the thing. That's the truth, and it was no picnic feeling either."[2]

In the ensuing battle that followed the Allied landing at Anzio, the 12th Air Force was made responsible for isolating the battle area and preventing the enemy from bringing up the reinforcements and supplies necessary for a successful counter-attack. In carrying out this assignment, the squadrons of the 79th Group including the 99th Fighter Squadron were assigned to support the ground troops by dive bombing and strafing rail yards, troop concentrations, highways, bridges, ports, and supply centers. However, hard luck continued to follow the 99th Squadron. The squadron on January 3, 1944, lost Lieut. John H. Morgan of Cartersville, Georgia, who died from injuries sustained in a crash while slow-timing his plane. Twelve days later on January 15, Lieut. William E. Griffin of Birmingham, Alabama, crash landed his plane in enemy territory after being hit while dive bombing. Upon landing, Griffin was captured by the Germans and held as a Prisoner of War until the end of the war.

The squadron could only show one victory at the completion of six months of combat duty. This was disheartening and the morale of the 99th was far from high. To make matters worse, the ground crewmen had just about lost faith in their pilots' courage to engage the enemy.

The opportunity to prove that they were capable pilots presented itself on the morning of January 27, 1944. A flight of twelve planes, led by Captain Clarence Jamison of Cleveland, Ohio, spotted a group of enemy fighters over the Anzio beachhead. Desperate for victories, the flight broke formation and went after the enemy planes. They met the enemy at all angles and refused to give ground although they were outnumbered almost two to one. This was a desperate group of men determined to gain victories or die trying. This was the opportunity they had prayed for; therefore, they had to make the best of it. The battle didn't last long, but in less than five minutes they had knocked down five of the enemy aircraft. The remaining enemy pilots, seeing that they were fighting a losing battle, turned tail and headed for home.

As the victorious and happy pilots returned to the field their morale was high. They buzzed the field several times and each made a victory roll before landing. This was the biggest day in the Squadron's history. The morale of the whole squadron, pilots and ground crewmen, reached a new height and the victorious pilots were heartily received. The pilots credited with victories were as follows: Lieuts. Willie Ashley Jr. of Sumter, South Carolina; Leon Roberts of Pritchard, Alabama; Robert W. Diez of Portland, Oregon; Edward L. Toppins of San Francisco, California, and one victory between Howard L. Baugh of Petersburg, Virginia, and Clarence Allen of Mobile, Alabama.

All twelve of the planes returned safely. Major Roberts' plane had a huge hole torn in its left wing. Lieut. Henry Perry of Thomasville, Georgia, was hit by an 88-shell that ripped a hole in his left wing. The plane of Lieut. Pearlee Saunders of Bessemer, Alabama, developed engine trouble on the mission and was forced to return to the base. Lieuts. Walter Lawson of Newton, Virginia, and Albert Manning of Spartanburg, South Carolina, also participated in the mission.

Another patrol flight over the Anzio beachhead was led by Lieut. James T. Wiley on the afternoon of the same day. A flight of FW-190s escorted by ME-109s enemy fighters was sighted by the patrol as soon as it arrived in the Anzio area. With the morning's victories still fresh in mind the pilots vigorously attacked the enemy formation. In the battle that followed Captain Lemuel R. Custis of Hartford, Connecticut, Lieuts. Charles Bailey of Punta Gorda, Florida, and Wilson Eagleson of Bloomington, Indiana, shot down three more enemy

Fig. 9. CAPTAIN CHARLES B. HALL

Fig. 10. AIRPLANE ARMORER, SGT. CONWAY WADDY

Fig. 11.   GROUND   CREW   OF   THE   99TH   FIGHTER
SQUADRON

aircraft, which brought the total of victories to eight for the day.

Lieutenant Samuel Bruce of Seattle, Washington, was the only casualty listed for the entire day. He was last seen chasing two Focke-Wulf 190s and therefore had to be considered missing in action. Lieut. Allen G. Lane of Demopolis, Alabama, was forced to bail out of his plane, which was set afire by a flak burst. He landed safely near an airfield at Nettuno and returned to the base two hours later in a Cub plane piloted by Staff Sergeant William R. Lynn of Millbury, Massachusetts. A third pilot, Lieut. John A. Gibson of Chicago, Illinois, was forced to crash land his plane when he returned to the base because his hydraulic system had been damaged by flak.

At the end of the day the victorious pilots were anxious to relate their experiences. They had a large audience. Captain Lemuel Custis, commenting on their success, said: "It was the roughest day of the campaign, but the hunting was good all the way." Major "Spanky" Roberts remarked: "We've been looking forward to such a happening, but this is the first time in five months that we have encountered enemy opposition. The whole show lasted less than five minutes. It was a chasing battle, as the Germans were always on the move. We poured hell into them." Lieut. Leon Roberts, describing his victory, said: "I was following and was weaving a lot, but I got a burst into his right wing and he flopped over on his back and dived into the ground." Lieut. Willie Ashley remarked: "I saw a Focke-Wulf 190 and jumped directly on his tail. I started firing at close range, so close that I could see the pilot. After blasting away with all my ammunition, I saw the enemy plane smoking and fire flaming from its left side." At this time Lieut. Howard L. Baugh of Petersburg, Virginia, entered the conversation. "I saw twelve or more Focke-Wulf 190s cut away from our ships and hit the deck. I was flying about 5,000 feet and went down firing. I gave three or four bursts of fire, then saw one plane skid along the tree tops, throwing clouds of dust as it hit the ground."

The Allied Air Force had one of its best combat days in the

Italian campaign on January 28. Fighter planes protecting the Anzio beachhead knocked twenty-one enemy aircraft out of the sky, while Flying Fortresses raiding Southern France destroyed fourteen enemy planes. In the two days of fighting Allied fighter planes destroyed eighty-five and Allied bombers destroyed fifty enemy planes. During the battle on January 28, Captain Charles B. Hall destroyed two enemy aircraft, Lieuts. Robert W. Diez of Portland, Oregon, and Lewis C. Smith of Los Angeles, California, shot down one each. On returning to the base the victorious pilots were congratulated by Major General Joseph Cannon, Commanding General of the 12th Air Force.

Despite the aerial losses over the beachhead, the Germans continued to send over large forces of aircraft in an effort to halt the Allied all out drive. Seventeen planes were engaged over Anzio on February 5, by a flight of seven led by Captain Clarence Jamison of Cleveland, Ohio. Although outnumbered over two to one, the flight destroyed one of the enemy planes. Lieut. Elwood T. Driver was credited with the only victory.

While Lieut. Driver was gaining his victory Captain Jamison and his wingman Lieut. George McCrumby were having trouble. Lieut. McCrumby's plane was hit by an ack-ack burst and went into a dive at 4,000 feet. Lieut. McCrumby related: "I tried to pull out, but had no control of my elevators. Seeing that I had lost control of my plane I tried to climb out the left side of the cockpit, but the slip stream knocked me back into the plane. Then I tried the right side and got half way out when the slip stream caught me and threw me away from the plane where I dangled until the wind turned the ship at about 1,000 feet from the earth, shaking me loose. I reached for the ripcord six times before finding it. My parachute opened immediately and I floated to a safe landing in a cow pasture."

The broadcast of the celebration of the third anniversary of Tuskegee Army Air Field, August 9, 1944, was the occasion for Captain Jamison to relate his story. "It was over Anzio beachhead. I was leading a flight of seven planes that day. We'd been up a short time when we got word over the radio that a flight of seventeen Focke-Wulfs were coming at us. When we saw them they were too high for us to catch until they'd dropped their bombs, and then we closed in. I took off after four of them, when all of a sudden my guns jammed. A Focke-Wulf got on my tail, and I couldn't shake him off. I dropped on deck and hedge hopped along, but he chased me ten or fifteen miles before he lost me. By that time he had hit my engine and I knew I had to get out of there. I tried to climb high enough to jump, but I couldn't make it. So I made a crash landing. I didn't know just where I was, of course, but when I found I was all in one piece I began to look around. I saw three American paratroopers motioning to me. I was only 200 yards from the German line and 300 yards from our forward position."

The success of the 99th Squadron brought an official commendation from General Arnold. It read: "The results of the Ninety-ninth Fighter Squadron during the past two weeks, particularly since the Nettuno landing, are very commendable. My best wishes for their continued success."

The 99th Squadron was credited with three more victories on February 7, when Lieuts. Wilson V. Eagleson, Leonard M. Jackson, and Clinton B. Mills were each credited with an enemy aircraft. Lieut. Jackson, a slender Texas lad, related: "On February 7, 1944, during the hot Anzio battle I scored my first victory. I was patrolling over the beachhead in a formation of eight P-40s. The mission had been uneventful for forty-five minutes, then it happened. Sixteen FW-190s came over to dive bomb the Anzio harbor. The enemy was sighted and called in by our ground control. We saw the enemy planes dive as our flight passed heading south. As the Focke-Wulfs pulled out of their dive, they turned into our tails. Three members of our four ship element, which included Lieuts. Eagleson, Knighten, C. B. Mills, and myself, pulled around into a tight 180 degree turn. As the turn was initiated the Jerries broke away and started climbing. I was on the right side and turned away from my element leader into the enemy. On recovery from the turn,

I observed a Jerry plane pulling away from my plane. I gave him one burst at 150 yards and another at about 200 yards. I was about to break off my attack when I saw the Jerry plane turn over and tumble to the ground. I expected him to pull out and come back after me, but the ship continued to plunge earthward. The pilot bailed out of the damaged plane at 1,500 feet."

Late in January, 1944, the United States 34th Division managed to break through the northern end of the Gustav line. The French Corps simultaneously captured key hills east of Mount Cairo, which dominated the Cassino area. An attack was launched on the heavily defended town of Cassino by the Allies on February 1, 1944. Support for the ground troops was again supplied by the 99th Squadron. The elaborate fortifications and an estimated 100,000 men of Marshal Kesselring, Commander of the German forces, could not stem the Allied tide. The hills to the north and northwest of the famous Hill 516 on which stood the ancient Benedictine monastery were captured by the Allies after twelve days of fighting. All attempts by the Allied ground forces, however, to take the town were repulsed by the Germans, even though the 12th Air Force had plastered the town with bombs. On February 13, the 79th Group flew 131 sorties against German strongholds, supply dumps, and troop concentrations.

Early in February the New Zealand Corps of the Eighth Army, together with the Fourth Indian Division, relieved the Second Corps of the Fifth Army. They were assigned the mission of capturing the town of Cassino. The New Zealand Corps managed to take roughly one-third of Cassino but, due to bad weather, it was forced to postpone its assaults.

Meantime misfortune struck the 99th again on February 21, 1944. Lieut. Alwayne W. Dunlap of Washington, D.C., was killed as his plane crashed when he overshot a landing strip on the Anzio beachhead. Nine days later on February 29, Lieut. George McCrumby was reported missing in action. While on a mission Lieut. McCrumby pulled out of his formation near

[54]

Geata Point. He radioed that he was returning to the base because his plane had developed engine trouble. He was never
seen or heard from again.

As of February 10, 1944, the 79th Fighter Group victories
were as follows:

SQUADRONS	DESTROYED	PROB. DESTROYED	DAMAGED
85th	29	8	11
86th	17	2	9
87th	41	7	24
99th	17	4	6

CHAPTER VIII

THE 99th FIGHTER SQUADRON AND OPERATION STRANGLE

During the lull in the fighting at Cassino plans were made for an all out spring offensive against the enemy. It was believed that the enemy's ability to supply, reinforce, and shift his forces could be so weakened that he could neither withstand determined ground attacks nor withdraw in an orderly way. Using these views as a central theme, Allied Air Force Commanders developed and put into effect a plan known as "Operation Strangle." Needless to say, the aim of "Operation Strangle" was to reduce the flow of enemy supplies far below requirement.[1]

While the ground troops rested and prepared for the spring campaign, the Mediterranean Air Force, commanded by Lieut. General Ira C. Eaker, was active. It plagued communication and supply lines far up the peninsula and harassed enemy troops in the Cassino area.

The Allied ground forces together with the Air Force opened their spring campaign in March, 1944, with an assault on Cassino. A terrific aerial bombardment by more than 500 planes, including planes from the 99th Squadron, practically levelled Cassino. When the New Zealand Corps tried to advance, it found roads so cratered and choked with debris that tanks could not be used. The stubborn Germans fought off all attempts to take Cassino, and as a result, General Alexander, the Allied Commander, was forced on March 23, 1944, to call off the battle.

From March 24 until the fall of Rome on June 4, 1944, the Allied Air Force kept up a continuous attack on the enemy forces. Two interdiction lines were maintained across Italy

[56]

which prevented through trains from running from the Po Valley to the front lines. This forced the Germans to move practically all their supplies south of Florence by truck.

The enemy attempted to use ships to bring in supplies, but heavy bombers attacked the key ports and coastal aircraft attacked the vessels. The enemy resorted to motor trucks to haul supplies around the broken bridges and eventually all the way from Florence to Rimini. This operation, however, could only be carried out at night because Allied strafing made any daylight attempt impossible.[2]

Meantime the pilots of the 99th Squadron were kept active. On March 23, the 99th struck gun positions east of Anzio and Nettuno. Gun positions north of Ardea were the next to be attacked on the following day by the Squadron under the leadership of Lieut. Walter Lawson. On March 25 a flight from the 99th dive-bombed targets in the Palestrina area. During the mission Lieut. Clarence Dart's ship was set afire by a flak burst. He rode his plane down from 12,000 feet and landed in friendly territory.

The squadron suffered a casualty on March 28, 1944, when Lieut. Edgar L. Jones of New York City was killed. While taking off on an early morning mission, Lieut. Jones' plane collided with several parked planes on the side of the runway. Two days later Lieut. John Stewart Sloan of Louisville, Kentucky, was shot down by enemy ack-ack guns as he pulled up from dive-bombing a target in the Cassino area. Shrapnel pierced the bottom of his plane and fractured his upper thigh bone. Immediately after being hit, Sloan called his element leader, Lieut. Robert W. Diez of Portland, and reported that he was badly hurt. A little later, Sloan's plane got out of control. He bailed out of his crippled plane and landed safely. The following day he returned to his base.

Throughout the month of March, 1944, the 99th Fighter Squadron fighting with the 79th Fighter Group supported Allied ground troops in the Cassino and beachhead areas. During the month the group flew one hundred and seventy-two missions. However, at the end of March the 99th Squadron was released from operations with the 79th group as a result of the Group's reassignment to bomber escort duty.

The 99th Squadron moved to Cercola, Italy, on April 1, 1944, and was attached to the 324th Fighter Group. Upon arrival at its new base, the Squadron was reorganized and Captain Erwin B. Lawrence of Cleveland, Ohio, succeeded Major Spencer Roberts, who returned to the States.

Shortly after receiving his appointment as commanding officer of the 99th, Captain Lawrence addressed the Squadron. He said, "I am happy to have a bunch like you to work with me. You are all good men. We will try to live up to the record made by the squadron under our two former leaders, Colonel Davis and Major Roberts, and if possible, to continue to improve. It will be tough for me to follow in the footsteps of these men, but I will do my best."

Throughout the month of April, 1944, the 99th dive-bombed and strafed enemy positions in the Anzio and Cassino areas. The success of the squadron was expressed by General Ira C. Eaker, Mediterranean Allied Air Force Commander, when he inspected the squadron on April 20. He said "By the magnificent showing your fliers have made since coming to this theatre and especially in the Anzio beachhead operation you have not only won the plaudits of the Air Force but have earned the opportunity to apply your talent to much more advanced work than was at one time planned for you."

The sustained offensive by the Air Force practically eliminated the use of rail transportation by the Germans. They resorted to the use of motor trucks for long supply hauls, but they were unable to build up significant reserves.

Around the first of May, 1944, preparations were made for the spring offensive against the enemy. Air and Ground Forces were given two complementary objectives. The Mediterranean Allied Air Force was assigned to the mission "to make it impossible for the enemy to maintain his forces on its present line in Italy in the face of a combined Allied offensive." The

Ground Forces were "to destroy the right wing of the German 10th Army; to drive what remains of it and the German 14th Army north of Rome, and to pursue the enemy to the Pisa-Rimini line, inflicting the maximum losses on him in the process."[3]

On May 11, 1944, the big drive against the enemy began. The Fifth and Eighth Armies charged forward. The 99th also went into action as support for the ground troops. On D-Day, May 11, it flew thirty-one sorties and dropped 30,000 pounds of bombs on enemy positions. However, the Squadron suffered a casualty when Lieut. Neil V. Nelson of Amarillo, Texas, and Chicago, Illinois, failed to return from a mission. He was last observed pulling into formation after making his bomb run. According to pilots who made the mission, visibility was so poor in the target area they were forced to pick their way through the clouds. This factor and the high concentration of flak they attributed as the probable cause of Nelson's failure to return from the mission.

The following day the 99th flew twenty-eight sorties against a bridge spanning a valley between the Germans north of Cassino and German supply dumps. During one of the missions Lieut. Elwood Driver's plane was severely damaged by flak, but he was able to nurse the ship back to the base. Lieut. Theodore Wilson of Roanoke, Virginia, was forced to bail out of his ship when it was damaged by a flak burst. Fortunately, however, Lieut. Wilson landed in a hospital area and was able to secure another plane to fly back to his base.

The coordinated operations of the Air Force and Ground Forces worked as planned. The enemy's night convoys were unable to meet the added requirements for rapid movement of troops and materials to the front. Desperate for supplies the enemy attempted to use his motor transports in daylight convoys. These convoys were extremely vulnerable to Allied Air attacks, and as a result the enemy suffered heavy losses, both in troops and supplies. The enemy's line broke under the impact of the air and ground offensive. The Germans were unable to withdraw in an orderly way because of their disrupted transportation system. Within a week, General Clark's Fifth Army surrounded Cassino, and on May 17 the town was captured.

General Mark Clark complimented the 99th Fighter Squadron on May 16 for the support it gave his ground troops. The citation read: "For contributing materially in forcing the German units to surrender to advance Allied infantry in the current all out offensive." Major General John K. Cannon, Commanding Officer of the Twelfth Air Force, also praised the 99th as "battle hardened and one of the most experienced in giving close air support to ground troops in the entire theatre of operation."

The pilots of the 99th were told on May 22 that the second phase of their campaign against the enemy would start at 6:30 A.M. on the morning of May 23. The Anzio beachhead was to be expanded and the battle line would be continued from the Fifth Army bomb line until the beachhead forces and the Fifth Army met. The 99th's immediate mission was to strike targets northwest of the beachhead and south of Rome.

As planned, the Anzio garrison burst from its confines on the morning of May 23, 1944. In a wild battle at Cisterna the Allied Forces repelled seven German counter-attacks and took the town. Later the Anzio troops were joined by the Fifth Army which came up the West Coast. Together they pursued the retreating German 14th Army which fell back to protect the Alban Hills and the city of Velletri.

The 99th flew an armed reconnaissance mission northeast of Lake Albano on May 26. During the mission Lieut. Woodrow Morgan developed engine trouble. He landed by mistake on an enemy airfield located west of Frosinone and was seized as a prisoner of war. Lieut. Robert Diez, who covered the disabled pilot, was hit several times by enemy gun fire but was able to return to his base. A third pilot, Lieut. Alva Temple, had his rudder shot out, elevators practically shot off, and large holes ripped in his fuselage. In spite of these damages, Temple landed his plane safely at the base.

General Mark Clark sent the following message to the

Twelfth Air Force headquarters on May 27: "Greatly pleased with splendid effort of Air Force. We have put the enemy on the road. Good hunting to all." The next day the 99th continued its attack on the enemy by dive-bombing in the vicinity of Frosinone. Though the squadron effectively carried out its assignment one of its members, Lieut. James B. Brown of Los Angeles, California, failed to return from the mission. Lieut. William H. Thomas, relating what happened to Brown, said: "Brown went down in the lower layer of clouds which was about 1,500 feet. A pilot flying in a rear element saw a plane dive through the clouds and later heard Brown cry out that he had been hit. Lieut. Dart went down below the clouds and saw Brown's plane hit in a forest area and skid about fifty feet. He didn't see J. B. get out. He saw some peasants around the plane. Later, however, it was picked up in a prison camp that J. B. was captured by the Germans and marched away. But while marching down the street J. B. was hit by American artillery shell fire. Some Allied Intelligence officers found J. B.'s dog tags and underwear."

On June 1, the Germans were forced to retreat from their stronghold in the city of Velletri. With their Alban Hill defense broken the Germans retreated to Rome. Two days later, Allied troops entered Rome and forced the Germans to retreat from the city. Following the capture of Rome, General Clark on June 5 stated that the 12th Air Force support "had enabled us to show the enemy how irresistible the Air-Ground combination can become."

The capture of Rome was the occasion of celebration throughout the world. To the soldiers, however, it marked only a milestone back to the States. The Germans were on the retreat and it was not time to let them rest.

The 99th Squadron flew armed reconnaissance north of Lake Braccino on June 5. The next day it strafed vehicles on a highway between Lake Bolsena and Lake Vico. During the assault, Lieut. Leonard Jackson's plane was severely damaged by flak. Seeing that he could not keep his plane in the air, Jackson glided across Lake Braccino and landed in a wheat field. As he climbed out of his ship he was greeted by a small band of American soldiers. The soldiers had recognized the American plane and had come up hurriedly to offer assistance. Jackson learned that the soldiers were volunteers sent out to search a house for snipers.

While Jackson talked with the search party, he noticed two German soldiers waving a white flag from a ravine. He motioned them to approach and took their arms. Jackson turned the Germans over to the search party and then proceeded to Rome. Here he was interrogated and returned to the squadron.

Lieut. Clarence Allen of Mobile, Alabama, was also shot down by flak during the mission. He landed in enemy territory but managed to hide himself before the Germans reached him. The entire area was sprayed by machine gun fire when Allen refused to surrender. Several attempts were made by the Germans to force Allen from his hiding place, but all failed. Seeing that their efforts were not successful, the Germans gave up and departed.

The next morning Allen crawled out of the cave and found that he was less than one hundred feet from a German machine gun nest. That afternoon, an American tank squad entered the area and forced the Germans to move. Circumstances being very favorable, indeed, Allen decided to make a break. His efforts to reach friendly territory were met with success. He was able to reach a camp of French soldiers after sliding down a whole mountain side. Exhausted from his hazardous trip, Allen collapsed before he could identify himself. He was revived and carried to the French headquarters. Here he was questioned and given physical examination before being returned to his squadron.

Fate seemed to have been against Allen. A week later on June 14 he was again shot down. This time it was a strafing mission over Southern France. Again he was lucky. He escaped being taken by the Germans. Upon arrival at the base he was returned to the States.

Meantime on June 8, 1944, the 99th lost Captain Lewis C. Smith, who was shot down by small arms fire while dive-bombing and strafing. After bailing out of his disabled plane, Smith was set upon by a mob of angry civilians. He was rescued by a squad of German soldiers who carried him to Florence, Italy. Ten days later he was shipped to Frankfort on the Main. Not long after this he was moved again to Sagan, Silesia, where he remained until January 22, 1945. At this time he was transferred to Stalag Luft 7-A. in Moosburg, Germany. Smith was held prisoner here until liberated by the Allies on April 29, 1945.

The capture of Rome placed the Germans in a strategically vulnerable position. They fell back in good order to defenses 150 miles north on the Arno river. The weary enemy troops were given no respite as the Allied ground and Air Forces continued to press them. The 99th joined the 86th Fighter Group at Ciampino, Italy, on June 11, and immediately went into action dive-bombing and strafing enemy troop concentrations and strongholds in the Rome area. On June 12, the squadron strafed in the Rome area where it encountered heavy flak and machine gun fire. It dive-bombed a bridge at Macchie on the 15th and on the following day dive-bombed and strafed in the San Quirico area.

The 99th moved to Albinia on June 20, 1944, with the 86th Fighter Bomber Group. Here it went into action dive-bombing and strafing in the Florence-Pisa area. On the 21st the squadron dive-bombed a railroad east of Pisa. The next day it continued its attack. From the 23rd to the 27th of June it dive-bombed railroads northeast of Florence.

On June 29 the 99th was sent to the Po Valley to knock out some 500 railroad cars. Heavy concentrated flak greeted the squadron as soon as it reached the Po area. Lieut. Floyd Thompson was hit by flak burst which severely damaged his plane. He was forced to bail out of his plane in the vicinity of Florence.

He was taken prisoner by the Germans and held until the end of the war.

Lieut. Charles Bailey of Punta Gorda, Florida, became excited when heavy flak burst rocked his ship. Thinking his plane was damaged, he requested escort back to the base. Lieut. Herber C. Houston of Detroit, Michigan, was assigned to escort Bailey on the return trip. Checking his ship after landing at the base, Bailey found it was not damaged as badly as he thought. Only a few small flak holes were found in the wings and tail assembly.

July 2, 1944, was the last day on which the 99th flew as a separate unit. It was on this day that the squadron which had ended operations with the 86th Fighter Group on June 29 and moved to Orbetello, Italy, left to join the 332nd Fighter Group. The next day the 99th joined the 332nd at Rametelli, Italy, and was immediately integrated into the group.

The Allies took Siena on July 3, and on the 19th, Polish troops captured Ancona on the Adriatic. Meanwhile, British troops, advancing through central Italy over difficult terrain, passed around both sides of Lake Trasimeno, took Arezzo, and opened up the road to Florence. The Germans retreated to the Pisa-Florence-Rimini line where they prepared for an all out offensive.

CHAPTER IX

THE 332nd FIGHTER GROUP

Originally, the 332nd Fighter Group consisted of three Squadrons, the 100th, 301st, and 302nd. Shortly after entering combat, however, the group was enlarged by the integration of the 99th Squadron.

The 100th Fighter Squadron was the first of these to become active. Under the leadership of Lieut. Mac Ross of Dayton, Ohio, the 100th was activated at Tuskegee on May 26, 1942. Lieuts. George L. Knox and Charles Debow, both from Indianapolis, Indiana, were assigned as adjutants of the newly formed squadron. The Squadron remained at Tuskegee until March 27, 1943, and was then transferred to Selfridge Field, Mt. Clemens, Michigan, as a component of the 332nd Fighter Group.

Changes in officer personnel were made in July of the same year. Lieut. Mac Ross now became the Group Operation Officer. The promotion of Mac Ross left the squadron without a Commander. This vacancy was quickly filled by the appointment of Lieut. George Knox as Squadron Commander. Lieut. Elwood Driver took over the command in December, 1943, but his assignment lasted only a week. He was succeeded by Lieut. Robert B. Tresville, a graduate of the United States Military Academy. In June, 1944, Lieut. Tresville failed to return from a mission. Lieut. Andrew D. Turner of Washington, D. C., then became the squadron leader. He commanded the squadron until hostilities ceased in the European Theatre. When Turner returned to the States, Captain Roscoe Brown of New York City was appointed. Captain Brown commanded the squadron until it returned to the States in October, 1945.

The 301st Fighter Squadron was activated at Tuskegee in

the early part of 1943. It, too, like the 100th, had a series of Squadron Commanders. Captain Charles Debow was the first to fill this position. During his command, the squadron was ordered overseas. Captain Debow was relieved of his command in April, 1944, and Lieut. Lee Rayford of Ardwick, Maryland, replaced him.

Lieut. (Major) Rayford was returned to the States after completing his tour of duty and Major Armour C. McDaniel of Staunton, Virginia, took over the command. A change in command was again necessitated when Major McDaniel was shot down over Berlin in March, 1945. Captain Walter Downs then became the new leader and held this position until the outfit returned to the States at the close of the war.

The 302nd was the last of the group to be activated. This occurred in March, 1943, under the leadership of Lieut. William T. Mattison of Conway, Arkansas. This particular unit of the group, however, encountered adverse conditions. In the beginning, the unit was considered only a pool for the other two squadrons. Most of its personnel, both officers and enlisted men, were considered the least desirable members of the group.

The seeming disregard of the ability of the members of the 302nd, however, played a very potent part in welding it into a capable and effective outfit. The men realized that whatever they did wrong would reflect on the squadron and at the same time substantiate opinions about their characters and abilities. They were determined to do everything a little better than the other squadrons of the group. The 302nd began demonstrating its possibility as a fighter unit on maneuvers in the North woods of Michigan. Here the squadron developed the team spirit that it carried into combat.

Late in the summer of 1943 Lieut. Mattison was replaced by Lieut. Robert Tresville. Tresville commanded the squadron only a short time before being transferred to the 100th Fighter Squadron. Lieut. Edward C. Gleed of Lawrence, Kansas, succeeded Lieut. Tresville and carried the squadron overseas. On April 10, 1944, the squadron received a new Commanding

Fig. 12. CAPTAIN LEONARD JACKSON IS DECORATED

Fig. 13. MAJOR WILLIAM T. MATTISON

Fig. 14.   PILOTS OF THE 332ND FIGHTER GROUP

Fig. 15.   PILOTS OF THE 332ND FIGHTER GROUP
BEING BRIEFED BY COLONEL DAVIS

Officer, Lieut. Melvin T. Jackson of Warrenton, Virginia. He commanded the squadron until he returned to the States in the spring of 1945. Captain Vernon C. Haywood, the next Commander, carried out his duties until the squadron was deactivated in March, 1945.

Although the first squadron of the 332nd was formed in May, 1942, the group was not officially activated until October 13, 1942. On that date Lieut. Colonel Samuel Westbrook was appointed to command the 332nd, and plans for actual organization began. A month later on November 13, 1942, the first cadre of enlisted men was transferred from the 318th Base Headquarters and Air Base Squadron at Tuskegee to the group.

The 332nd Fighter Group under the command of Lieut. Colonel Samuel Westbrook was transferred to Selfridge Field, Michigan, on March 27, 1943. But the stay at Selfridge Field was brief for the majority of the Group's personnel. On April 13, 1943, the 100th Fighter Squadron moved from Selfridge Field to Oscoda, Michigan, for a temporary change of station. The 301st Fighter Squadron followed on May 5, 1943, and by May 21, 1943, most of the Group had moved to Oscoda, Michigan, with the exception of radio mechanics and other technicians of the 302nd Fighter Group who remained at Selfridge Field. The 302nd, the last of the fighter squadrons to be activated, did not have sufficient line personnel to function as a unit at Oscoda. Consequently, only the pilots of the 302nd Fighter Squadron underwent the initial training phases conducted at Oscoda, Michigan.

Colonel Robert R. Selway Jr. took over the command of the 332nd in June, 1943. Under his direction the group was reorganized and an effective training plan put into action. Intensive training in combat tactics was given by Lieut. Richard Suer, veteran of the Aleutian Campaign.

The instruction given by Lieut. Suer did not fall on barren soil. Within a comparatively short period of time the 332nd developed into a combat unit whose motto was summed up in the slogan, "Get to your damn guns," adopted by Colonel Selway.

The training program at Selfridge Field, however, was not without casualties. Shortly after it went into training at Selfridge the 332nd lost one of its most popular pilots in the death of Lieut. Sidat Singh. A native of New York, he had already gained national recognition for his participation in football and basketball at Syracuse University long before entering the army.

After completing his studies at Syracuse University, Singh moved to Washington, D. C., where he became a member of the Metropolitan Police force. It was during this time he played professional basketball with the famous "Washington Bears." By his superior playing he was instrumental in leading the "Bears" to the National Professional Basketball Championship.

Singh enlisted in the Air Corps on August 7, 1942, and was sent to Tuskegee as an aviation cadet. On March 25, 1943, Singh was commissioned as a Second Lieutenant in the Air Corps and sent to Selfridge Field where he became a member of the 332nd Fighter Group. While flying over Lake Huron on a routine training mission on May 9, 1943, the engine of Singh's plane burst into flame. No alternative being possible, he bailed out of his ship into the water. Forty-nine days later his body was recovered by a coastguardsman and turned over to the group.

After nine months of intensive training the 332nd Fighter Group was considered ready for combat. On October 5, 1943, Colonel Benjamin O. Davis assumed command of the group and immediately made preparations for combat. He was assured of experienced leaders when Captain Louis Purnell, Captain Lee Rayford, Lieut. Elwood Driver, and Lieut. Graham Smith reported to the group on December 2, 1943. These men had served their tour of duty with the 99th Fighter Squadron and had volunteered to return to combat with the 332nd Fighter Group.

On December 23, 1943, the 332nd was transferred to the Port of Embarkation at Camp Patrick Henry, Virginia. Here the members of the 332nd received their final processing before embarking for overseas duty on January 3, 1944.

[68]

CHAPTER X

THE 332nd FIGHTER GROUP ENTERS COMBAT

The destination of the 332nd Fighter Group was no longer a secret. After three weeks of sailing, the first ship carrying personnel of the 301st and 302nd Squadrons arrived at Toranto, Italy. Other ships of the convoy arrived intermittently until February 3, 1944, when the final ship landed. Meantime, the 100th Fighter Squadron under Captain Robert Tresville landed at Naples, Italy, where it set up camp at the Capidachino Airport. Here it went into action on February 5, flying a coastal patrol mission to Naples Harbor under the leadership of Captain Andrew Turner of Washington, D. C.

A few days after the final convoy ship disembarked at Toranto, the 301st and 302nd Squadrons moved by truck to Montecarvino. Here the 332nd replaced the 81st Fighter Group which had performed coastal patrol and was being transferred to Burma.

After spending a short time at Montecarvino the 302nd Squadron and Group headquarters moved to the Capidachino Airport in Naples, Italy. The 301st Squadron under Major Lee Rayford remained at Montecarvino supporting ground troops fighting in the Anzio area.

The entrance into combat on the part of the 332nd was quite unlike that of the 99th Squadron. Almost immediately the group encountered enemy aircraft. On February 18, Lieut. Lawrence D. Wilkins of Los Angeles, California, and his wingman, Lieut. Weldon K. Groves of Edwardsville, Kansas, sighted a TU 88 near Ponsa Island off Gaeta Point. They chased the enemy aircraft as far as the Anzio Beachhead and were successful in getting several bursts into the enemy plane before they were forced to turn back because of a shortage of gasoline and a faltering gun.

Lieut. Roy N. Spencer of Tallahassee, Florida, and his wingman, Lieut. William R. Melton of Los Angeles, California, encountered an enemy reconnaissance plane near Ponsa Point about two days later. They sprayed the enemy ship with volleys from their guns, but failed to make the kill. Lieut. Spencer's guns jammed just after he had lined up the enemy aircraft and prepared to fire. Lieut. Melton took up the attack, but he was unable to make a direct hit on the enemy plane that maneuvered to keep from being shot down.

No battle has been fought without some casualties and the battle waged by the 332nd was no exception. On February 24 a flight of four engaged in a routine training mission ran into a bad storm while flying over the Adriatic Sea. Lieut. Harry J. Daniels of Indianapolis, Indiana, was reported missing in action when he failed to return to the base. He was last seen trying to fight his way through heavy walls of clouds that closed in on his plane. Lieut. Ulysses Taylor of Kaufman, Texas, was forced to bail out of his ship after losing control. He was rescued by an Allied vessel and carried ashore where he was hospitalized and treated for severe shock received from hitting the water.

The group lost Lieut. Clemenceau Givings, a member of the 100th Squadron on March 18, 1944. Returning from a mission, Lieut. Givings' plane spun into the Adriatic Sea. His body was recovered by an Italian fisherman and on March 19 was laid to rest in an American Cemetery near the Capidachino Airport.

Lieut. John B. Quick, the Intelligence Officer of the 100th Squadron, said the last words over the body. As the burial party stood around the grave with heads bowed in silent prayer, Lieut. Quick said:

"There are some men in an outfit that you always expect to find around. 'Wild Bill Walker' was one, Clem Givings was another. Givings, the latest of our group to meet his death, was perhaps the most unique personality among us. He was strictly Air Corps, incorporating in his decorum all the zest, cock-sureness, pride, and braggadocio that is the essence of a fighter pilot's makeup. He was always talking about flying, about women, about everything a dare-devil talks about, and while he talked, we all listened. We had to; his voice was loud and never faltered for lack of words, and his speech was as colorful as a night full of ack-ack. To him, being a pilot was a great achievement and, to rate with him, one had to have wings. Well, he's gone now. The squadron has lost its first pilot in combat. While he lived, he lived a symbol of the Air Corps, and dead he is no less."

During a training mission of May 28, 1944, the engine in the plane of Lieut. Roger B. Brown of Glencoe, Illinois, conked out while he was flying 2,000 feet above water. After unsuccessfully attempting to start his engine, Brown found himself only 800 feet above the water and falling too fast to jump with his parachute. He jettisoned the doors of his ship, unfastened everything he could, cut off his switches, placed his hands over his gunsight, and held his plane off the water until his air speed was less than 120 miles an hour. When his ship hit the water he abandoned it in less than three seconds. Yet, despite his swiftness in getting out, the tail of his fast sinking plane struck him.

Lieut. Brown was rescued by a British vessel shortly after he abandoned his plane. For this accomplishment he was officially commended for being the first pilot of the United States Air Force known to have successfully crashed landed a P-39 Aerocobra at sea.

In spite of the casualties suffered by the 332nd, it effectively carried out its assignments of coastal patrol dive-bombing and strafing in support of ground troops fighting in the Rome area. When the 12th Air Force and Bombers denied the enemy the use of rail transportation and enemy motor convoys could not bring in ample supplies, the Germans resorted to the use of ships to bring in the much needed supplies. The 332nd together with other coastal Air Force units made these attempts unsuccessful. The Germans' supply problems were rendered so acute that when the Allies finally started the push on Rome Marshal Kesselring was unable to halt the drive. On Sunday, June 4, 1944, the Allies entered Rome and forced the Germans to retreat northward.

Even before the fall of Rome it had become apparent to Allied Commanders that the network of roads over which the Germans transported supplies and the supply centers further north and in Southern France had to be destroyed. Strategic bombing of these roads, bridges, enemy coastal ships, harbor installations, and supply centers was decided upon as the most effective means of crippling the German war machine. As a result many Tactical Fighter Groups were relieved of tactical operations and assigned to strategic bomber escort duty. The 332nd was one of the groups affected by this operational change. On May 31, 1944, it was transferred from the 12th Tactical Air Force to the 15th Strategic Air Force and assigned new P-47 Thunderbolt planes for escort duty.

CHAPTER XI

THE 332nd AND THE FIFTEENTH AIR FORCE

The capture of Rome gave the Allies added incentive to attempt an invasion of western Europe. On June 6, just two days after the conquest of Rome, the long awaited assault on the coast of France was launched. While the invasion of western Europe was taking place the battle of Italy was being accelerated. The Allied strategy in Italy was to keep the enemy forces fully occupied so that it would be impossible to withdraw any troops from Italy to help defend the coast of France.

The capture of Rome also held special significance for the Mediterranean Allied Air Force and, more specifically, for the Twelfth and Fifteenth Army Air Forces. It marked the culmination of the largest scale Tactical Air Force campaign to date and the emergence of strategic bombing as an important Air Force strategy in the Mediterranean theatre.

One of the main objectives of the Italian campaign was to capture the Foggia plains. Army Air Force planners had long recognized that Southern Italy could be used as bases for bombers to strike at the Balkans and at the industrial plants moved by the Germans beyond range of the British base bombers.

In September, 1943, Foggia was captured by the British Eighth Army. Almost immediately afterwards engineers began developing and repairing the numerous fighter plane bases that the Germans had constructed in the area. However, the fact that the bases had been built for lighter aircraft and the damages suffered by continuous bombings made it impossible for the Allies to make immediate use of the bases for bomber operations.

The Fifteenth Air Force was activated on November 1,

[73]

1943, and immediately went into operation on a small scale against enemy production centers. Meantime, throughout the winter of 1943, new groups were crossing the Atlantic to join the new Air Force. By April, 1944, the Fifteenth Air Force had grown to such an extent that it was ready for large scale operations. Fifteenth Air Force bombers and Fighters were sent to attack strategic targets beyond working range of the British based bombers. It was obvious, however, from the beginning that the success of strategic operations depended on a degree of air superiority, providing freedom for the heavy bombers to fly over enemy territory. The Germans had converted the aircraft industry to fighter production and moved it as far from the British based threat as possible—Bavaria, Austria, and Hungary. The 15th Air Force met opposition from these enemy fighters in its attacks on the production centers and suffered a large number of casualties.

The assignment of the 332nd to bomber escort brought the pilots in contact with more enemy aircraft and gave them a chance to register more aerial victories. A fighter sweep to the Po valley on June 7, led by Colonel Davis, was the first assignment of the 332nd with the 15th Air Force. The next day the group escorted bombers to Pola Harbor. Both missions, however, were uneventful in that no enemy aircraft was encountered.

The first big day of the 332nd with the 15th Air Force came on June 9, 1944. The group was assigned to fly top cover for heavy and medium bombers to the Munich area. On approaching the Udine area four ME-109s were observed making attacks from 5 o'clock high on a formation of B-24s. As each enemy aircraft made a pass at the bombers it fell into a diving turn to the left. Lieut. Wendell Pruitt of St. Louis, Missouri related:

"As the Jerries passed under me I rolled over, shoved everything forward, dove and closed in on one ME-109 at 475 miles per hour. I gave him a short burst of machine gun fire, found I was giving him too much lead so I waited as he shallowed out of a turn. Then I gave two long two-second bursts. I saw his left wing burst into flame. The plane exploded and went straight into the ground, but the pilot bailed out safely."

Lieut. Frederick Funderburg of Monticello, Georgia, sighted two ME-109s four hundred feet below at 9 o'clock. He peeled down on one of the enemy ships and fired a burst. He noticed pieces flying off the enemy ship as he continued in his dive. Then he made a steep climbing turn and found two ME-109s coming head on at him. He flew straight towards the Germans and fired until one of the enemy ships exploded.

Meantime, Lieut. Robert H. Wiggins saw a ME-109 coming at his level. He turned into the enemy plane and fired a burst. His fire found its mark, the enemy plane began to smoke and fell into a shallow dive. However, a few minutes later it gained speed and pulled away from Lieut. Wiggins who was attempting to follow up his attack.

Lieut. Melvin "Red" Jackson, relating how he got his victory, said "We were flying P-47 Thunderbolts. Colonel Davis was leading. Over the Udine valley Colonel Davis observed a group of ME-109s coming in on our bombers. Skipper called in that enemy fighters were attacking. 'Go get them.' Immediately I peeled off, out of formation and with my wingman following, went back to the scene of engagement. I noticed about seven ME-109s coming in at 5 o'clock, so I radioed my flight to drop belly tanks and prepare for attack. Then I fell in behind the second enemy aircraft which was coming down in string formation. Having a faster plane than the enemy I overshot him. However, my wingman, Lieut. 'Chubby' Green, and Lieut. Bussey, who were behind me, shot the enemy ship down.

"When I pulled out of my dive I started to climb. I noticed a ME-109 headed straight down at me, blazing away with all his guns. At the same time my plane seemed to be dragging on the climb, so instantly I realized that I hadn't dropped my tanks. I tried to drop them but they were stuck. Then I applied my water booster. This gave me additional speed and enabled me to pull away from my attacker.

"Below were the Alps with their high peaks, and just above a mountain top hung a layer of clouds. So finding myself hindered by the wing tanks, I decided to drop out of the battle and seek refuge among the clouds. I dived into the clouds, but as I broke out into the clear on the south side of the Alps I found my pursuer waiting to shoot me down. He made a pass at me, but somehow he missed. I fell in behind him. Realizing I was on his tail he began weaving from side to side. Every time he turned I gave him a short burst of fire. On the fourth burst his plane began to smoke. I saw the canopy come off the ME-109 in two pieces. A little later I saw the pilot jump and his parachute open. I circled the helpless pilot for a while. But looking down I saw that I was directly over an enemy airfield. I dove down on deck and headed for the Adriatic Sea. About ten miles out I gained altitude, settled down and cruised home happy over my victory."

The 332nd was credited with five victories during the mission. The victories were credited as follows: Lieuts. Frederick D. Funderburg, Monticello, Georgia, two ME-109s; Melvin T. Jackson, Warrenton, Virginia and Wendell O. Pruitt, St. Louis, Missouri, one ME-109 each; Charles M. Bussey, Los Angeles, California, and William W. Green, Staunton, Virginia, shared credit for destroying a ME-109.

Lieut. Cornelius G. Rogers of Chicago, Illinois, failed to return from the mission. Lee Rayford of Ardwick, Maryland, was wounded when his ship was badly damaged by a flak burst. The plane of Willie "Drink" Hunter of Albany, Georgia, was literally shot from under him by flak. When he arrived at the field he called his crew chief and remarked, "Horse, how about putting a few patches on our gal?"

Throughout the month of June, 1944, the 332nd escorted bombers to targets in Italy, Southern France, and the Balkans. On June 24 the 332nd was assigned to make a low-flying mission over water to strafe the Aircasea-Pinerolo landing ground located a mile and a quarter west of Aircasea, Italy. This was considered to be one of the most important enemy supply lines.

On the morning of the mission the group was briefed to fly very low over the Tyrrhenian sea to Corsica. This was designed to avoid being picked up by enemy coastal radar equipment.

The mission was carried out as planned until the group reached a point about thirty miles from the coast of Corsica. At this point Lieut. Charles B. Johnson, a member of the 100th Squadron, who was flying No. 4 position in the third flight of planes, developed engine trouble. When the engine cut out the plane, flying just above the water, almost immediately hit the water. He pulled his ship up a litle, but it failed to catch up. This time Johnson made a beautiful belly landing, but he forgot to open his canopy before hitting the water. The ship sank so rapidly Johnson could not get out.

Shortly after Johnson went down Captain Tresville made a slight turn. Because Tresville was flying so low, the rear flights were forced to pull up to avoid collision when he made the turn. The 100th Squadron led by Captain Tresville was flying beautiful formation and as yet no one in the lead squadron knew that Johnson had gone down.

As the flght skirted low over the water it met with another accident. Lieut. Earl Sherrod of Columbus, Ohio, permitted the belly tank of his plane to hit the water. He tried to pull up but the heavy tank pulled the plane down and caused the wing to hit the water.

Seeing that he could not get his ship up again, Sherrod quickly got out of the ship, walked out on the wing, pulled off his "chute" and inflated his dinghy. A few seconds later the plane sank below the surface of the water.

On seeing Sherrod's plane hit the water, Samuel Jefferson, who was flying to the right of Sherrod, made a tight 180-degree turn and attempted to circle the helpless pilot. But in making the turn a downward slip stream caught his ship and threw it into a flat spin. It crashed, exploded, and, in burning, left a huge cloud of black smoke.

Not long after Lieut. Jefferson went in, the flight reached the coast of Europe, between Southern France and Italy, approximately sixty or eighty miles above the spot where the flight was to dive-bomb. Somehow, on the initial turn Captain Tresville had turned east when he should have turned due north. Upon becoming aware he was flying off course Tresville made a 90 degree turn and flew up the coast of Italy, about ten miles off shore.

The 100th Squadron was still flying very low. This fact made those who flew the mission conclude that Tresville was still unaware that he had lost several men. They reasoned that if he had been aware of the accidents he would have pulled up higher above the water. Lieut. Spurgeon Ellington, who flew opposite Tresville on the mission, related that Tresville was glancing at his map when his plane slid off course and plunged into the water. On hitting the water, the plane was completely engulfed by a huge wave. After travelling under water about fifty feet it emerged above the water, pulled up above the water, slipped over a plane piloted by his wingman, Lieut. Dempsey Morgan, and fell back into the water.

Immediately after Tresville went down, Lieut. Woodrow Crockett, the deputy flight commander, took over. He continued the mission but, unable to find a break in the weather suitable to approach the target, he decided to return to the base.

When the Group returned to the base, it found four members, Captain Tresville, Lieuts. Samuel Jefferson, Charles B. Johnson, and Earl Sherrod were missing. However, Lieut. Sherrod was rescued by a British coastal ship and returned to the base the same day.

The casualties suffered on the mission affected the morale of the members of the 332nd greatly. Lieut. Carl E. Johnson of Charlottesville, Virginia, wrote to the wife of Lieut. Charles B. Johnson:

"My dear Isabelle,

I cannot express to you how hard it is for me to write you at this time. You know that there is much in life that we do not understand, the ways of man, the movement of the elements and strange ways of God. Yet he is my one and only hope now.

"This week will live in my heart and memory in infamy. Your great and heavy loss has been mine. I cannot tell you how deeply hurt I am. He meant more to me than a brother. I would like to express my deepest and most sincere sympathy to you and your family at this hour and time in our lives.

"It will perhaps help some if I should say that he is not known to be lost. There is still a faint hope that he is still alive. But in the annals of war, time makes a record. However, you must believe that the War Department will continue to make every effort to ascertain his whereabouts. The entire squadron maintains a hope and prayer that all is well. Yet if such is to be his case to give life, remember that he gave it in the line of duty, faithful and obedient to his mission against odds of battle and elements. This is all I can say . . . Today a storm rages. It touches every little brook, every river, every nook. Yes, even the far distant edges of the sea. But tomorrow—the sun, isn't it bright."

In spite of the tragic mission and the great losses suffered by the 332nd Group there was no hesitancy on the part of its members to carry the battle to the enemy. On June 25 the Group was assigned to strafe some roads in northern Italy, which were known to be the enemy's main supply routes for troops fighting in sections further south. At the briefing, Captain Joseph Elsberry, who was to lead the flight of twelve planes on the mission, was told that there were a large number of enemy troops coming out of Yugoslavia to reinforce lines in northern Italy. The flight was briefed to fly to Ancona, a port city on the Adriatic Sea, and fly over the water up the coast of Yugoslavia until it reached its target zone in the Pola area.

After the briefing the flight took off and headed for Ancona. On reaching Ancona it skirted low over the Adriatic and turned north towards the Pola area. However, the wind was stronger than the pilots had contemplated, and without realizing it they were blown off course into Trieste Harbor.

As the planes roared over the harbor the pilots spotted a vessel. At the briefing the pilots were told that they would find no Allied vessels in the area so they were at liberty to shoot at any vessel sighted. At first sight the vessel looked like a small American destroyer, but as the flight approached the ship they saw that it was an enemy ship. By now, the ship's crew, realizing that they had been spotted, began to open up with all the ship's guns and hid the vessel beneath a thick layer of black smoke. Lieut. Henry B. Scott, relating the battle that followed, said: "The flak was so thick when the destroyer opened up it looked like a blanket. It was throwing everything it had at us and, at 9 o'clock in the morning, it was so dark you'd think it was midnight."

Captain Elsberry led the attack with Lieuts. Henry B. Scott, Joe Lewis, and Charles Dunne following at close intervals After they attacked and pulled up, Wendell Pruitt and Gwynne Pierson went in. Capt. Pruitt made a direct hit that set the ship afire. Lieut. Pierson followed and made another direct hit that caused the destroyer to blow up, scattering debris so high into the air that his plane was almost knocked out of the sky.

After the victory the flight continued to its target area but on arrival sighted no troop movement. It circled the area for a while thinking maybe the enemy had camouflaged its movement. Unable to observe any activity, Captain Elsberry decided to return to the base.

On the way back to the base Lieuts. Joe Lewis and Charles Dunn flew up and down the coast of Italy shooting at everything they saw. Suddenly they sighted twelve enemy planes in the distance, but before they could radio the rest of the flight, Lewis' plane was hit by a flak burst that damaged his instrument panel. He tried to fly back to the base, but was forced to land before reaching the field. Lieut. Dunne circled the disabled ship until it landed, then after pin pointing its location returned to the base. Later a command car was sent out to pick up Lewis.

The news of the victory was received with great joy by the

members of the 332nd. After the pictures of the battle with the destroyer were developed Capt. Pruitt was credited with making a direct hit on the ship, but Lieut. Pierson was officially accredited as being responsible for the sinking of the ship. As a result of this victory both pilots were awarded the Distinguished Flying Cross in a ceremony which took place later.

The following day, on June 26, the 332nd was assigned to provide penetration escort for bombers which were to strike in the Lake Balaton area. Although the mission was successfully carried out, the group lost two pilots. Lieut. Andrew Maples Jr. was forced to bail out of his ship when it began to act up in the vicinity of Termoli. A second pilot, Lieut. Maurice V. Esters, was forced to bail out in the vicinity of Vetachandrija. Neither of the pilots was ever seen or heard of again.

Lieut. William Faulkner, a close friend of Lieut. Maples, wrote to Mrs. Maples:

"My dear Mrs. Maples,

By now you must have received word that Andy is missing, and I feel you undoubtedly would like to know whether it is true, how it happened, and the possibilities of his coming out safely.

"On the morning of the mission, he was scheduled to lead a flight of four ships, one of which was mine. Because of engine trouble, I was unable to take off with him, but the rest went on.

"After about fifteen minutes, he called that he had developed mechanical trouble and was returning to the base. Since he was close to base, his wingman did not return with him, but continued on with the formation.

"A few seconds later he called in that he was bailing out and a fix (by radio) was taken on his position. Some of the men in the squadron following his formation saw his plane strike the water about five miles from shore in the midst of about a hundred small Italian fishing boats. None saw a parachute.

"All of this, of course, was on this side of the front

line. When I learned that he had bailed out, I got two fellows to go with me over the water to look for him. For three hours, the limit of our planes' endurance, we searched a fifty-mile radius about the point down on the water, but saw no rubber boat, no parachute, no oil slick. Since then we've heard nothing.

"At first we thought he might have parachuted down near a fishing boat and he'd return in a couple of days. After four days passed we considered maybe he was being cared for by a fisherman's family, which may still be the case. There is also the possibility that the fisherman was a Fascist and took him up to the German side or he may have become entangled with the plane and gone down with it."

The victories and tragedies of the 332nd Fighter Group seemed to follow the pattern of a river tide. When the tide was in the Group registered a series of victories. When the tide was out the Group registered a series of tragedies. On June 28, the 332nd lost two pilots, Lieuts. Edward Laird of Brighton, Alabama, and Othel Dickson of San Francisco, California. Lieut. Laird died from shock when his plane spun into the runway at Rametelli while taking off on a routine mission. Lieut. Dickson was killed when he attempted to slow roll his plane over the Rametelli Airport. The death of Lieut. Dickson was typical of many casualties suffered by young, eager pilots during the war. He had just arrived overseas and was taking transition training when he met death.

While a cadet at Tuskegee he had won recognition as a promising combat pilot. He was acclaimed top aerial gunner of the Eastern Flying Training Command and third best cadet gunner of all Army Air Force cadets at a meet held at Eglin Field, Florida. These honors made him the envy of all cadets of his class and to maintain this recognition as a "hot pilot" he took unnecessary chances which finally led to his death.

Meantime the ground battle had progressed. The defeat on the outskirts of Rome placed the Germans in a strategically

Fig. 16.   BRIGADIER GENERAL DAVIS DECORATES
PILOTS OF THE 332ND

Fig. 17.   PILOTS OF THE 332ND DECORATED WITH
THE D. F. C.

Fig. 18. MAJOR McDANIEL, CAPTAIN FRIEND, AND
CAPTAIN DRIVER

vulnerable position. Unable to halt the Allied drive, the enemy retreated northward to the Pisa-Florence-Rimini line, along the Arno river. Here it dug in and prepared for an all out defensive campaign.

CHAPTER XII

THE 99th JOINS THE 332nd FIGHTER GROUP

The retreat of the German army to the Pisa-Rimini line set up a new problem for the Allied Mediterranean Air Force. "Operation Strangle" had cut the rail lines in central Italy on a route by route basis, but the complexity of the rail system in the Po valley precluded any operations of similar scope in the north.

To cope with the new problem, a division in the assignments of the Strategic and Tactical Air Forces was instigated. The Tactical Air Force was assigned to cut and keep cut all lines supplying the German front. The Strategic Air Force was assigned to hit the marshaling yards in northern Italy, southern France, and Germany beyond the reach of the Tactical Air Force. The new plans also called for a large scale determined ground attack to force the enemy to use up, at a very fast rate, whatever supplies he had left. This was an operation designed to make the enemy "burn both ends against the middle."[1]

Meantime new developments were taking place that affected the 332nd Fighter Group. The 332nd was transferred to a new base in Rametelli, Italy. On July 3, 1944, the 99th Squadron, which had previously been attached to the 86th Fighter Group, joined the 332nd at Rametelli.

The transfer of the 99th to the 332nd Group brought new problems. The members of the 99th were satisfied being attached to the 86th Fighter Group, though it was an all white outfit. When the 99th received orders to join the 332nd, many of the 99th's members felt that the War Department was reverting to segregation policies practised in the States. The pilots of the 99th who had fought with tactical outfits ever since entering combat felt that color and race should not be used as a basis for

[84]

transferring the unit to a strategic outfit. On June 1, 1944, the late Captain Edward Thomas of Chicago, Illinois, wrote in his diary: "We received orders to join the 332nd Fighter Group today and everyone is unhappy."

Colonel Davis also met operational difficulties by the transfer of the 99th to the 332nd. A fighter group as a rule consists of three squadrons. When the 99th joined the 332nd plans had to be made for the extra personnel. This required a great deal of extra planning and reorganizing. Many of these changes brought dissatisfaction and unfavorable comments. Lieut. Colonel George S. Roberts, relating the situation, said: "Colonel Davis and I saw the condition and immediately endeavored to eradicate it. When the actual combining of the units took place I was in the States. When I got back and actually saw the jealousy among the men, I felt ashamed of my race. The members of the 99th hated to lose their identity by being integrated into a larger unit. They imagined themselves with fifty or more missions flying as wingmen for men who had no combat experiences. On the other hand, the members of the 332nd Fighter Group feared the experienced pilots of the 99th would be assigned to all the responsible positions. Anyway, we set about to integrate the units and it took us about three months to do it. We who tried to straighten out the matter, stuck our necks out and were scorned by members of the 99th. However, we finally got the men together as a team."

Not long after the 99th was integrated into the 332nd Group, Captain Mac Ross of Dayton, Ohio, was killed. The death of Mac Ross aggravated the strife between the members of the two organizations. Mac Ross, a rather reticent lad, was one of the most conscientious workers of the Group. Shortly after winning his wings at Tuskegee Army Air Field he was appointed as commanding officer of the newly activated 100th Fighter Squadron. He was relieved of his assignment before the Group embarked for combat and appointed as Group operation officer. When the 332nd entered combat, Mac Ross served as principal pilot of a C-78 which was used as the Group's business transport plane. This assignment kept him busy and as a result he received very little combat experience.

The job of Operation Officer required an experienced man. Colonel Davis realized that the success of the Group depended largely on effective operations. Therefore, he relieved Mac Ross of his assignment and appointed Lieut. Alfonso W. Davis of Omaha, Nebraska, a pilot with two years combat experience as operations officer. On July 11, shortly after being relieved of his assignment, Mac Ross was killed while taking transition training in one of the Group's newly acquired P-51 Mustangs. It was alleged that Mac Ross was very despondent over being relieved as operation officer and his mind was not on flying when he flew his fatal mission.

The Group suffered another loss in the death of Captain Leon Roberts of Pritchard, Alabama. Captain Roberts at the time of his death was operation officer of the 99th Fighter Squadron. He was the youngest member of the original 99th Squadron and had completed 116 missions. Captain Edward Thomas noted in his diary: 'Captain Roberts crashed and was killed. He was operation officer for the 99th. A damn good pilot, too. Think altitude got him. He was about 30,000 feet, peeled away from formation, and wasn't seen again until his wrecked plane and remains were found."

In war, a combat unit cannot take time out to mourn the death of its members. Death is accepted as routine. This was true in the 332nd as in all other combat units. Though the 332nd lost two of its members on July 11, the next day it was in the air again. On July 12, the Group escorted B-17s of the 5th Bombardment Wing to southern France to bomb a marshalling yard. During the mission, pilots of the 332nd were attacked by a formation of enemy fighters. In the ensuing battle, Captain Joseph D. Elsberry of Langston, Oklahoma, shot down three of the enemy aircraft and Lieut. Harold E. Sawyers of Columbus, Ohio, shot down one enemy plane.

Lieut. Sawyers, a tall, handsome lad, was a proud pilot when he returned to the base. Relating how he scored his victory, he said: "The weather was so bad our group was the only group able to get through. Near the target we were jumped by twenty-five enemy aircraft. After three of the enemy aircraft had attempted to attack the bombers Lieut. 'Bernie' Jefferson and I followed them down. I pulled up behind one of the enemy planes and got a burst into its tail section. Immediately the enemy plane began making split S's while diving towards the ground. I followed the enemy until I saw him crash."

In every combat outfit during the war there were certain men that stood out as having unusual amount of "guts". Captain Joseph D. Elsberry, without a doubt, was one of these men. This slender youth possessed a competitive spirit that would not allow him to be satisfied with defeat. This was the man that three unfortunate German pilots tried to do battle with on the morning of July 12, 1944.

When the flight took off the weather in the immediate vicinity of the base was bad and the ceiling was less than 12,000 feet. On the take-off Captain Elsberry, who was assigned to lead the Group, instructed the flight leaders of the 302nd and the 100th Squadrons to take their squadrons up separately in small units over the overcast. Elsberry figured that it would be too risky to have so many planes flying on the same level in such bad weather. This, however, required a relatively long time and resulted in the squadrons being approximately forty miles apart.

During the take-off several members of the 100th Squadron got lost in the overcast and not being able to locate their flights returned to the base. One member of the 100th, Lieut. George Rhodes, developed engine trouble and was forced to bail out of his plane in the vicinity of Rome. He was picked up by friendly natives and taken by motorcycle to an English mission where he stayed until he received transportation back to his base at Rametelli. Lieut. Woodrow Crockett, another member of the 100th Squadron was unable to find his squadron. He joined up with a flight from the 301st Squadron and continued on the mission.

The 332nd reached the rendezvous point two minutes

late, but fortunately the bombers were five minutes late. This put the 332nd three minutes early. Finding that it was ahead of the bombers, the Group made a fast 360 degree turn and fell in over the formation and began to weave over the bombers. About three minutes later the formation crossed the coast of Southern France. Approximately ten minutes later it sighted a group of aircraft at a distance at 10 o'clock high.

As the fast approaching planes closed in, they turned in the direction of the bombers and came in on the bombers in a trail formation. On recognizing the planes as enemy aircraft Elsberry instructed his men to drop their auxiliary tanks and prepared for an attack. When the Jerries saw the tanks fall from the planes they turned away from the bombers. In turning they left themselves exposed to attacks from the rear. Seizing this break, the pilots of the 332nd pulled in behind the enemy planes and started firing.

Captain Elsberry opened fire on one plane at long distance. Although his shots hit the target he realized no results. Not long afterwards an enemy aircraft turned in front of Elsberry's plane. Elsberry gave his plane the gun (throttle) overtook the FW 190, pulled up behind it in a good shooting range, lined up his sight and fired away. A mild explosion occurred midway the fuselage of the enemy plane as a few short bursts hit the mark. A few more bursts sent the enemy plane into a roll and finally it wandered off to the right and headed downward to earth.

Just after Elsberry finished destroying his first plane a second enemy plane crossed in front of him, reefing at a 70-degree bank. Immediately, Elsberry rolled in on the enemy and fired 80 or 90 degrees around a turn. The enemy plane began to smoke and fell into a dive towards the ground.

A third enemy plane shot down across Elsberry's plane at about 45 degrees. Elsberry rolled his ship to the left, followed him and started firing. When he began firing, the enemy plane broke into split S's to evade Elsberry's guns. Elsberry followed him down to about 11,000 feet, then looking back noticed four planes of the 332nd following closely behind. Elsberry broke off his attack and joined his comrades. The enemy pilot, thinking he was still being followed, continued his dive. Just before reaching the ground he attempted to pull his plane up, but the plane crashed into the ground.

The 332nd flew its first four squadron escort missions as protective cover for the 15th Air Force heavy bombers on July 15. On July 17, the 332nd provided penetration target cover and withdrawal for the 306th Bomb Wing which had been assigned to bomb the Avignon marshalling yard and railroad bridge. Approximately nineteen enemy aircraft were seen in the target area. Three of the enemy planes attempted to intercept the bombers and were shot down. Credit for the victories was given to Lieuts. Robert H. Smith of Baltimore, Maryland; Luther Smith of Des Moines, Iowa; and Lawrence D. Wilkens of Los Angeles, California. However the most interesting story of the mission was told by Lieut. Maceo Harris of Boston, Massachusetts. He related:

"My flight leader and I went down on two bogies and after they split S'd from me at about 18,000 feet I pulled up all alone in a tight chandelle to the left. I tried to join another ship, but lost him when I peeled off on two more bogies which were after some bombers. The bogies seeing me coming in on them turned steeply to the left. Seeing some P-51s in the vicinity I decided to stay with the bombers because they were now hitting the target. Flak was intense over the target. I kept an eye for the enemy planes that might come in when the bombers left the target area.

"Upon leaving the target, I joined another P-51 and tried to contact him by radio. My attempt was unsuccessful, so I peeled off alone on three bogies who were approaching a bomber from the rear. At first they looked like P-51s so I rocked my wings, but as they swung left away from the bombers I could see they were enemy aircraft.

"I circled the bomber because the top turret gunner was firing on me. Finally he recognized me and stopped firing. I came in very close to survey the flak damage. The number two engine was feathered and the number one was smoking moderately. I could receive the bomber on channel A, but he could not receive me because my signal strength was one.

"We used the sign language and I conveyed to the pilot the info that he should not crash land on the French coast since his number one engine looked as though it would hold out for a while. I used five fingers to show the fellows that we'd be in Corsica in forty minutes and they understood perfectly. Their compass was out, so I put them on course and brought them into 'Black Top' at Corsica. My radio was out so I buzzed the field several times to clear the runway. They landed O.K.— partly on their belly. Only the tail gunner was injured. They took him out on stretchers. The B-24 pilot was from San Francisco. He is in the 459th Bomber Group and his ship number is 129585. He and the co-pilot appreciated my friendly aid and kissed me several times after the manner of the French."

Early in the morning of July 18 the 332nd took off to escort bombers of the 5th Bomb Wing to Memmingen airdrome. As the formation approached the Udine and Treviso areas it was attacked by 30 or 35 ME-109s and FW-190s. In the encounter the Group shot down eleven enemy planes and damaged another. The most successful pilot of the mission was Lieut. Clarence D. Lester of Chicago, Illinois, who was credited with three of the victories. The other members of the Group who gained victories were: Lieuts. Jack Holsclaw of Portland, Oregon, two; Lee Archer of New York City, one; Walter J. Palmer of New York City, one; Edward L. Toppins of San Francisco, California, one; Charles P. Bailey of Punta Gorda, Florida, one; Hugh S. Warner of New York City, one; Roger Romine of Oakland, California, one; Andrew D. Turner of Washington, D. C. severely damaged an enemy aircraft, but was unable to confirm his victory.

The 332nd victories, however, were not gained without losses. Three of its members, Lieuts. Oscar D. Hutton, Wellington G. Irving, and Gene C. Browne, failed to return to the base with the rest of the flight. Lieut. Hutton was last seen flying northeast of Venice headed towards the base. Lieuts. Irving and Browne were lost in the Kempton area. However, Lieut. Browne landed safely in enemy territory and was held as a prisoner of war until he was freed by the American ground forces at the end of the war.

Lieut. Browne, a short, small built lad who looked more like a high school kid than a combat pilot, related: "I was chasing a ME-109 and had him lined up in my sights when another ME-109 stole up behind me and began to fire on me. Lieut. Joseph Gomer tried to warn me that the ME was on my tail, but I was so eager to make the kill his warning didn't register in my excited brain. My plane was so badly damaged I was forced to crash land.

"I was sent to Augsburg where I stayed two days. Then I was sent to Frankfort. I stayed there a day and a half, then was shipped to Wetzlar. I stayed there three days. From Wetzlar I was sent to Stala Luft 7-A near Munich. I was held there ten months. Here I also met several members of the Group, namely: Lieuts. Alfred Carroll, Sterling Penn, Griffin, Gould and several others."

The 332nd escorted B-24s of the 47th Heavy Bombardment Group to Friedrichshafen in the Munich area on July 20. On the morning of the mission, the sky was filled with heavy clouds and a heavy mist covered the airbase. In spite of the weather, the flight took off with success. On arriving at the rendezvous point over the Udine area, northeast of Venice, it sighted the bombers being attacked by a squadron of ME-109s. Immediately the 332nd dropped its wing tanks and started after the Jerries. The enemy planes were split S-ing from about 33,000 feet down on the bombers. At the time, the 332nd was at 29,000 feet and the bombers were at 27,000 feet.

Unable to intercept the enemy planes because of the enemy's advantage of altitude, orders were given to concentrate on the enemy planes as they started away from the bombers. One by one, the pilots of the 332nd fell in behind the Jerries as they left the bombers. Finally Captain Govan, the Group's

[91]

leader, seeing the bombers were being left without protection, ordered the pilots to return and cover the bombers.

Just as the flight led by Captain Joseph Elsberry reached the bombers a Jerry plane which had just completed its attack on the bombers, swept across Elsberry's plane. Elsberry immediately turned in behind the Jerry and at the same time called Captain Govan and reported he was following a "bogie" that he had lined up. After chasing the enemy a short distance he opened up with a few short bursts that hit the enemy ship. The enemy plane burst into flames, rolled over and started straight down.

At this point Elsberry looked back and saw another enemy aircraft between his plane and his wingman, Flight Officer Gould. Elsberry decided not to follow up the disabled plane because he was sure it was through. So yanking back on his flaps to about 35 degrees and making a turn and a quarter he fell in behind the Jerry. However, in the maneuver he had lost considerable altitude and, forgetting to turn on his defroster, ice formed on his windshield. Although his vision was impaired he was determined to make the kill. He chased the fleeing German for a distance, but before he could open fire he found himself running into a mountain peak. He was forced to pull up to avoid crashing, and in doing so, he lost his enemy who disappeared into the mountain. Relating his mission, Elsberry said, "This was the last time I engaged an enemy aircraft at close range and my failure to register this victory meant the difference of being cited as an ace."

In the meantime, while Elsberry was having his engagement, Lieut. Lee Archer attacked one enemy plane while Lieut. Charles Bussey attacked a plane. The plane Lieut. Bussey was following made a steep diving turn in front of Archer. Archer fell in behind it with Bussey following on his wing. They chased the enemy until he crashed into the side of a mountain after being hit by a volley from Archer's guns.

When the victorious pilots returned to the base after the mission they were as happy as a group of kids on Christmas morning. Lieut. Edward Toppins was as much elated over his third victory as was Lieut. Langdon Johnson over his first victory. Perhaps the happiest pilot of the Group was Captain Armour McDaniel, who had gained his first victory. McDaniel, a stocky built Virginian, who appeared older than he actually was, related how he scored his victory. "After Elsberry attacked the leader I attacked the leader's wingman. I couldn't catch him somehow, but glancing downward I saw another enemy plane trying to make its getaway. I dived on him, dropping from 27,000 feet to 10,000 feet. When I fired on him he dove through some clouds and crashed against a mountain. I pulled up just in time to miss crashing into the mountains."

CHAPTER XIII

STRIKING OIL

While the 332nd was engaged in the Italian campaign it was also taking part in the Allied Air Force offensive against German oil supply centers. As far back as 1940 the Royal Air Force struck specific oil targets in the Ruhr and elsewhere. However, it was not until the Allies had driven the Nazis out of Africa and gained limited air superiority that the smashing of Nazi refineries and synthetic plants could assume its rightful priority.

The principal German oil centers in Germany were the synthetic plants in the three main coal regions of Silesia, the Ruhr, and around Leipzig. Various coke ovens, gas works, and L. T. carbonization units added a little to the German oil supply, but by far the greater percentage of Germany's natural sources were scattered throughout the German occupied countries.

It was realized at the beginning of the oil offensive that an effective reduction of Nazi output called for neutralization of the Luftwaffe to permit a concentrated assault. There had been successful missions against the Nazi oil centers before 1944, notably the attacks on Ploesti oil fields in August, 1943, but the Nazi fighter strength was so strong that such missions could not be carried out without great losses. The Allied Air Force, therefore, concentrated on the demolition of aircraft plants, ballbearing factories, and related industrial installations. By May, 1944, this objective had been so effectively carried out that the Luftwaffe could not seriously interfere with Allied operations. Nazi single engine fighter production had been cut by more than eighty percent. The Germans also had lost thousands of their combat planes and many of their best pilots.

The field was now clear for an all out offensive against the

Nazi oil centers. The Royal Air Force was assigned to attack petroleum plants in the Ruhr. Central, northern, and eastern Germany, western Czechoslovakia, and western Poland was the area designated for the operation of the Eighth Air Force. The Fifteenth Air Force was to strike at Southern Poland, Austria, Hungary, Italy, Southern France, and the important Balkan countries including Romania.

The Germans made frantic efforts to reduce the vulnerability of their oil centers. For example, at Ploesti the oil region covered an area of nineteen square miles which was densely crowded with refineries and pumping stations interconnected with a railway network. In May, 1944, when the oil offensive began, heavy bombers went into action against the refineries. The Germans counteracted with active and passive defenses. Their fighters were sent up in force, with Romanian and Nazi pilots flying fast ME-109s. Anti-aircraft guns, including four-barreled 20MM, 88MM, 105MM, and 128MM, threw up protective curtains of intense and accurate flak.

Fighter interception and ack-ack were not the sole extent of Hitler's defense preparations. Beginning with the last Allied raid in May, 1944, the whole Ploesti area was screened by a thick swirling artificial fog. Approximately 2,000 smoke generators were employed and functioned every time Allied airmen came over.

Another defensive feature at Ploesti was the concentration of high blast walls. These walls were built around every installation at each refinery. Nothing quite like them had been seen. Some were six feet thick at the bottom and tapered upward to a height of twenty feet, where they were two feet wide. Even a series of three pumps had a complete square of blast walls around it, and from the air the whole arrangement had the weird, dazzled, painted appearance of a gigantic, one-story, multi-room roofless house.

In July, 1944, the 15th Air Force struck at oil targets and related installations seventeen days of the month. The 332nd Fighter Group shared in many of these missions. On July 4 it struck at Piteste, Romania. On July 8 it was over Vienna, Austria. It escorted bombers to the Ploesti oil fields on July 13, and took part in a fighter sweep to Vienna, Austria, on July 16. The Group was credited with two victories on July 16, as a result of the guns of Lieuts. Alfonso W. Davis and William W. Green.

Lieut. Eugene D. Smith, a member of the flight, related: "We were returning from the target at 28,000 feet when our flight leader, Captain Alfonso 'Preflight' Davis, spotted a lone B-24 bomber in trouble headed for home about 10,000 feet below us. He called the flight and said he would take the bomber home. Almost immediately after his call he rolled over into a vertical dive followed by Lieut. Green and myself. I didn't see immediately what he was after, but in a short order I saw two Macchi 202s starting a dive behind the bomber.

"Captain Davis gave chase and lined up the rear fighter, but he was traveling so fast he overshot it. He continued on to line up the first enemy plane. Lieut. W. W. Green took the last one and I followed Captain Davis. Captain Davis opened fire and the Macchi started smoking. However, Captain Davis was traveling so fast he was overtaking the enemy so he broke rather than overshoot. The enemy plane, however, had been badly damaged and went into the ground in a diving turn. Meantime. Lieut. Green got his plane and we returned home with two aircraft to our credit."

On July 21 the 332nd furnished withdrawal escort for bombers in the 15th Air Force's first mission to Brux oil refineries in Bohemia. The next day the Group escorted bombers to the famous Ploesti oil fields. The mission was carried out as planned, but, returning from Ploesti, Captain James Walker, the flight leader, was shot down over central Yugoslavia. Like many pilots on similar missions, he made the mistake of flying over a small town which looked harmless. Captain Walker's plane was so severely damaged that he was forced to bail out. He landed in friendly territory and was taken to an underground hideout by some friendly peasants. A few days later he was joined by a crew of nine white airmen who also had been shot down.

After remaining in the hideout a short while Captain Walker and the other airmen started out together for their respective bases. They covered three hundred miles, over rough and mountainous country, wading through snow and water, before they received transportation to their bases.

Captain William Faulkner of Nashville, Tennessee, led an escort mission to Linz, Austria, on July 25, 1944. On the way to the target, the bomber formation was intercepted by a group of thirty enemy aircraft. In the battle that followed, two members of the 332nd, Lieut. Alfred Carroll of Washington, D. C., and Lieut. Sterling Penn of New York were shot down. A third member of the Group, Lieut. John Leahr of Cincinnati, Ohio, was not so unfortunate, but he was a very disappointed pilot when he returned to the base. During the battle he was able to get two enemy planes lined up in his sights, only to be disappointed by the failure of his guns to fire. When he arrived at the base he found his gun heater had been improperly connected, causing his guns to freeze.

Captain Joseph D. Elsberry related, "the flight was about fifteen minutes from the rendezvous point when an estimated twelve enemy aircraft were sighted making vapor tracks about 11 o'clock high from the leading squadron. Captain Melvin Jackson called in that a group of bogies had been sighted. At the time we were weaving above our bombers, Lieut. Faulkner, who was leading an element of the 301st, immediately began spreading out and as a result was drifting away from the bombers. I called 'Bubble Blue leader,' the code name for the 301st, to come back over the bombers, that we were getting too far away from them. By this time the Jerries were close enough to be seen clearly and instead of twelve there were approximately forty of those S. O.B.'s. Lieut. Faulkner's element, however, was caught out by itself and the enemy diving from about 5,000 feet above knocked Lieut. Carroll's plane tail off with a 20MM shell and continued on in to attack the bombers. My

[97]

flight was still weaving above the bombers. The enemy then began lobbing 20MM shells into Faulkner's flight of eight planes. This forced Faulkner to turn back towards the Jerries in order to protect himself.

"In the meantime, Lieut. Faulkner began calling for me to join in the battle. There was so much confusion over the radio at the time that I couldn't hear Faulkner and instead of helping the distressed pilots I began to order them back into formation over the bombers. In the meantime Lieut. Sterling Penn was shot down.

"I consider this my luckiest mission. Several times when I saw Jerry dodging back and forward above me I felt like leaving my position with the bombers and going after them. But on the way back home I found out how lucky I was in not following my temptations. When I tried to drop my wing tanks I found them to be stuck. I tried to fire my guns with the hope of shaking them off, but to my surprise my guns wouldn't fire. Captain Cisco also told me later that there were two enemy planes following an aircraft that had dodged across me. If I had followed him I probably would have run into a lot of trouble, especially with no guns and two heavy wing tanks to hold me down."

Lieut. Harold Sawyer also vividly described the mission: "We were covering B-17s. After we intercepted the bombers each flight was assigned to cover certain portions of the bombers. Captain Faulkner was leading the Group. He also led a flight of four and I led a flight of four. We saw a group of MEs and decided that as long as they didn't attack us we wouldn't leave the bombers. They came in at 4 o'clock to 6 o'clock putting them behind us with altitude. As we climbed up they came down. About thirty jumped our flight of eight. I saw smoke rings over my canopy. We got into a tight luffberry. A little later I noticed one enemy aircraft coming in at 3 o'clock. Meantime, Lieut. Leahr called in that his guns were frozen. The enemy broke into us and immediately I started firing. I fed him a lot of rounds that damaged his ship severely and sent it into a spin. I couldn't follow him down as other enemy planes were still up there. A few minutes later Captain Faulkner called that the other bandits had gone. We then caught up with the bombers and continued on our mission."

The 332nd escorted heavy bombers to Vienna on July 26. Just before reaching the target the Group encountered a group of enemy aircraft which was sent up to intercept the bombers. The encounter that followed brought the 332nd more victories. Lieuts. Weldon Groves of Edwardsville, Kansas, and William W. Green of Staunton, Virginia, shared one victory. Lieuts. Freddie F. Hutchins of Donaldsonville, Georgia, Leonard M. Jackson of Fort Worth, Texas, and Roger Romine of Oakland, California, each received a victory.

Captain Leonard Jackson in relating the mission said: "We were escorting B-24s to Vienna when I got my second Jerry plane. Captain Edward Toppins was leading my flight when we sighted three FW-90s ten minutes before reaching the target. Captain Toppins turned into them and fired, but they were out of range for effective shooting. Toppins damaged one on the tail of the formation, then we reassembled in battle formation. Just then we sighted three ME-109s above us making vapor trails. We were at 28,000 feet. We climbed as the ME-109s started a gradual climbing turn. I knew Captain Toppins was not going to let them get away, so I prepared for a good fight.

"Their ships decreased in rate of climb and we gained altitude on them while climbing to 36,000 feet. We closed in on them, and I had an enjoyable feeling for it was the first time I had seen Jerry when he couldn't run away or outclimb me. When our ships closed in at 500 yards the Germans decided to quit the trail. The MEs pointed their noses toward the earth and began to dive. We reeled around and began to follow them. I gave a short burst at 150 yards, then we broke through a layer of stratus clouds at 20,000 feet. When we broke out of the clouds I saw a Jerry spinning and burning. As I pulled away I saw a second ME going down in flames, the victim of Captain Toppins' guns."

[99]

On the way back to the base after the mission the plane of Lieut. Charles S. Jackson Jr. of Chicago, Illinois, developed engine trouble while he was flying over Yugoslavia. Before bailing out of his ship Jackson radioed his element leader, Captain Lowell C. Steward of Los Angeles, California, and reported that he could not keep his ship in the air. Captain Steward circled Jackson until he landed safely, then returned to the base and reported the incident.

The next day the 332nd led by Captain Lee Rayford of Ardwick, Maryland, escorted bombers to Budapest, Hungary, to bomb the Mannifred Wiess Armonenof works. Over Lake Balaton the Group encountered a group of ME-109s. It was successful in destroying eight of the enemy aircraft. Captain Edward C. Gleed of Lawrence, Kansas, and Lieut. Alfred M. Gorham of Waukiska, Washington, each was credited with two enemy aircraft. Captain Claude B. Govan of Newark, New Jersey, Lieuts. Felix J. Kirkpatrick of Chicago, Illinois, Richard W. Hall of Albany, Georgia, and Leonard M. Jackson of Fort Worth, Texas, was each credited with a victory.

The all out offensive against Nazi oil producing centers reached its climax during the month of July, 1944. By the end of the month almost all of the important refineries and synthetic oil plants had been attacked by the Allied Air Force. Conservative estimates showed that the loss of output of the plants attacked between May and July, 1944, was in excess of 400,-000,000 gallons. By August, German gasoline production had been reduced to twenty percent of its minimum requirement.

The persistent bombing of Germany's oil industries had a costly effect on her war machine. The Luftwaffe was left without sufficient gasoline for training pilots. Panzer divisions were left stranded for lack of fuel, and civilian use of gas and oil was virtually prohibited.

CHAPTER XIV

THE INVASION OF SOUTHERN FRANCE

Early on the morning of June 6, 1944, more than four thousand Allied vessels steamed across the English Channel. A few hours later Allied troops successfully landed on the coast of France and quickly pushed inland. Within five days the Allies had landed sixteen divisions in Normandy. By June 12 the Allies controlled eighty miles of the Normandy coast. So rapid was the Allied advance that by June 18 the Americans had swept across the Cotentin Peninsula, established a corridor seven miles wide, and continued their advance to the outskirts of Cherbourg.

At Cherbourg the Allies met with stiff resistance. For five days the Germans fought off the American assaults. Finally, on July 25, the enemy was forced to retreat.

"When Cherbourg and the Cotentin Peninsula had been won, the Americans turned south, broke through the German left flank at Avranches, drove into Brittany, swung around and outflanked Paris from the South. Two weeks of savage fighting had won Saint Lo on July 18, opening the way to a breach of the German lines."[1]

Meanwhile the British Second Army fighting at Caen had also met success in its campaign against the Germans. The town of Caen was the pivot of the German Seventh Army in Normandy and the German Fifteenth Army along the channel coast to the east. The Germans therefore put up great resistance to hold Caen.

Even as the Germans were fighting desperately to withdraw their battered armies from Normandy and trying to pull out of Paris they were threatened with a new invasion from the south. The 12th and 15th Air Forces were in full force against enemy forces in Northern Italy and Southern France. While the 12th Air Force dive bombed and strafed Nazi supply lines and troops in Northern Italy, the 15th Air Force bombers and fighters kept the coast of France under continuous bombardment. In the week before D-Day, August 15, 1944, in Southern France, medium bombers knocked out all the enemy airdromes in the Po valley and with the aid of fighters carried out concentrated assaults on gun positions, radar stations, and Italian Rivieras.

The 332nd Fighter Group also took part in the preinvasion assaults. Pilots of the Group flew as escort for 15th Air Force bombers and dive bombed and strafed enemy supply trains, convoys and radar stations in the Toulon, Cannes, and Nice areas.

Bombers of the 15th Air Force were escorted to Southern France on August 6 and 7, by the 332nd Fighter Group. No enemy aircraft was encountered; however, the enemy attempted to drive off the invaders with heavy and concentrated flak. Another escort mission to Budapest, Hungary, on August 6 resulted in a victory for Lieut. Carl E. Johnson of Charlottesville, Virginia, who was credited with destroying a ME-109.

The most important pre-invasion assaults on Southern France by the 332nd came on August 12 and 14, 1944. On August 12, a flight led by Captain Alton F. Ballard of Pasadena, California, escorted bombers to Marseilles harbor to knock out coastal radar stations. Over the target the flight encountered dense and concentrated flak and machine gun fire. The radar stations were destroyed but in fulfilling its mission the 332nd lost several of its pilots. The pilots who failed to return were Lieuts. Alexander Jefferson, Langdon E. Johnson, Robert H. Daniels, Richard Macon, Joe Gordon, and Robert O'Neil.

Captain Woodrow Crockett, a tall, slender, quiet youth was one of the pilots who flew on the mission. He related: "We went into the target at about 15,000 feet. Then we began our dive on the target which was in Marseilles harbor. As we dived for the target the Germans began firing on us. Just as I ap-

[102]

proached the target my wingman, Lieut. Langdon Johnson, crossed in front of my plane and shot out to sea on deck. Instead of pulling his plane up he allowed his plane to hit the water. It hit, skipped two or three times, tearing off the plane's right wing, and sank below the water. I didn't see Johnson get out of the plane."

Captain Marion Rodgers, a rather modest Detroit youngster, vividly described the August 12 mission: "It was my first strafing mission. We went into the target area at 15,000 feet. I was number four man in the lead flight. Our leader brought us over the target, which were radar stations near the coast. Then he rolled his plane over on its back and went down on the target in almost a vertical dive. I had been nervous up to this time but when I started my dive it all left me. Now my attention was centered on bringing my ship out of the dive because it had gathered tremendous speed and the ground was rushing towards me. I still hadn't located the target. I was slightly to the right of the ship ahead of me and I saw him veer off to the right rather sharply, but I followed the other ships ahead of me while still pushing my own ship through a near split S.

"As my ship leveled out about 50 feet above the ground I had a glimpse of something that looked very much like the picture we had seen of radar stations. I had a chance to hold my trigger down for two seconds, then zigzagged out to sea on the deck.

"When I returned to the base I found out that our flight of eight had lost two ships, one of them being the ship that had veered to my right. I had no vision of the flak. I had thought there was none over the target area."

There are some pilots who survived combat by sheer luck or miracles. Such a pilot was Lieut. Richard D. Macon. Macon, a tall, slender, soft-spoken lad from Birmingham, Alabama, stated that an act of God saved his life. While participating in the mission of August 12, he ran into a cloud of flak that sliced his aileron controls and flipped his plane over on its back. The plane burst into flames and as he fought to straighten it out he

[103]

lost consciousness. While unconscious his body evidently slumped against the control stick and pushed it forward. This threw the plane into an outside loop and tossed him out of the plane. In some inexplicable manner the parachute opened in time to partly break his fall and he landed in a ploughed field.

When he regained consciousness forty-five minutes later he found himself looking at three Germans. He was taken to a field hospital where he was found to have a broken shoulder and a broken neck. The doctors set his shoulder but the invasion of the area by Allied troops forced the Germans to move before they could set Macon's neck.

Two weeks later Macon arrived in Sagan, Silesia, where he was placed in a hospital staffed by French personnel. Here his neck was X-rayed and set. Before Macon could recuperate from his injuries, the Russians forced the Germans to move out of Sagan. Macon with his neck in a cast was taken to Nürnberg. The advance of the American troops on Nürnberg forced the Germans again to move, this time to Moosburg. Here Macon was held until he was liberated by the American Army.

In spite of the losses suffered by the 332nd on August 12, the mission was successful. The enemy's radar stations were knocked out and one member of the Group, Lieut. George Rhodes, was credited with an aerial victory.

Rhodes, a Brooklyn youth, was a quiet, unassuming fellow. He loved to fly and throughout his tour of duty he exhibited courage that won the respect of those who flew with him. On one mission over Rome he was forced to bail out of his ship. Returning from another mission he was forced to crash land. A few seconds after he stepped out of his ship it burst into flames and exploded, scattering its wreckage over the runway.

Relating how he scored his victory on August 12, Rhodes said: "About forty enemy fighters came up after us. Two made passes at us as we were flying formation. I spotted them coming down and I turned to intercept one of them. I fell on his tail and followed him down from 15,000 feet to 4,000 feet. I closed in on him and shot his right wing off and he went into a downward spin. At this time I heard a lot of bombs dropping and suddenly realized I was all alone, so I pulled up to 25,000 feet and headed back for the base. During the battle I lost my wingman Lieut. Robert O'Neil. He landed in the hills of France. He joined a group of partisans and fought with them. Later he returned to the base and was immediately sent back to the States."

On August 15 a large Allied invasion army landed on the coast of Southern France and swept swiftly inland. By the end of the first week the two most important Nazi held cities, Toulon and Marseilles, were isolated, and on August 28 both were occupied. Meanwhile, the advance up the Rhone valley was being pushed at full speed. On September 3 the 36th Division reached Lyons. Eight days later, on September 11, the French 1st Armored Division took Dijon and in the vicinity of Somberon linked up with the right flank of General Patton's Third Army. Four days later the Southern France invasion campaign was completed when General Wilson, Supreme Commander of the Mediterranean expedition, transferred operations to General Eisenhower.

Meantime, while the Allied ground forces were advancing in Southern France the 332nd Fighter Group together with other groups of the 15th Air Force were kept active. They struck targets to the north of the retreating Germans. They harassed the enemy troops, destroyed bridges, marshalling yards, supply dumps, and communication centers. For example, on August 22 the 332nd was over Germany. On the 24th it struck at Genoa, Italy. It escorted bombers to Brno, Czechoslovakia, on the 25th and Blechhammer on August 27. August 28 found the Group over Tanneskole, Germany. On September 12 the Group was over Lechfeld and Blechhammer, Germany.

CHAPTER XV

STRIKING AROUND THE CLOCK

At the same time the 15th Air Force was participating in the Southern France campaign it was performing other important assignments. It was aiding the partisans in Yugoslavia, flying shuttle missions to Prussia, hammering axis ports in Greece, pounding the Brenner Pass, through which materials were flowing to the stubborn German Armies in Italy, participating in the oil blitz, and aiding the Russians by striking Balkan communications and strong points.

The multiple assignments of the 15th Air Force kept the 332nd Fighter Group active continuously. On August 6, while some flights of the 332nd escorted bombers to Southern France, other flights of the Group escorted bombers to Budapest, Hungary. During one of these missions to Budapest, enemy fighters attempted to intercept the bombers before they could drop their bombs. However, the Germans were driven off by fighters of the 332nd and Lieut. Carl E. Johnson of Charlottesville, Virginia, was credited with shooting down a ME-109.

The 332nd furnished escort for the 15th Air Force bombers on August 19, in an attack on the Ploesti oil refineries. On August 23 it escorted bombers to Austria to knock out an enemy airfield which stood in the way of the Russian advance towards Berlin. Just before the formation reached the target area it was intercepted by a flight of seven ME-109s. In the ensuing battle two members of the 332nd, Lieut. Luke Weathers and Lieut. William Hill, shot down one of the enemy aircraft.

The next day the 332nd returned to Austria. Again it encountered enemy fighters and added three more enemy planes to its list of victories. The victorious pilots were: Lieuts. John F. Briggs of St. Louis, Missouri; William H. Thomas of Los

Angeles, California; and Charles E. McGee of Champaign, Illinois.

On August 25 the 332nd escorted bombers of the 5th Bomb Wing over Germany. The mission, however, was carried out without resistance by enemy fighters. The next day the 332nd escorted B-17s and B-24s to the heavily fortified Ploesti oil fields. Although the mission was successfully carried out, Lieut. Henry A. Wise of Cheriton, Virginia, was forced to bail out of his ship which developed engine trouble on his return to the base.

The fact that Lieut. Wise volunteered to fight the Nazi is sufficient evidence of his fighting blood. In July, 1942, when the Allied chance of winning the war looked very dim, Wise volunteered for the Army. In spite of the numerous stories of Allied losses in the air he applied for cadet training. He was sent to Tuskegee Army Air Field where he earned his wings. In July, 1944, he joined the 99th Fighter Squadron and flew thirteen missions over France, Romania, Germany, and Italy before he was forced to parachute from his plane.

When the men returned to Tuskegee after the war, most of the evenings were spent "shooting the breeze" about combat experiences. Wise had his story to tell, and this is how he related what happened to him after bailing out of his ship on August 26: "Returning from the mission to Ploesti on August 26, I was forced to bail out of my plane at 9,000 feet. Immediately after hitting the ground I was captured by a group of Bulgarian soldiers and taken to prison. I was placed in a local guard house at the nearest enemy camp. I stayed there only two days, but in those two days I almost starved because I couldn't eat the type of food they gave me.

"On the third day I was placed under guard and carried across country to a prisoner of war camp. The camp was a lone stone building constructed to hold about 100 men. But already there were about 300 men at the camp, all Allied fliers, British, North Africans, Yugoslavians, Australians, Poles, and Americans. Officers and enlisted men were all encamped together,

[107]

dirty, hungry, and definitely in need of clothing because all of it had been taken when they were captured.

"I was the only Negro in the camp. However, I got along as well as the others and no difference was shown by the Bulgarians or my fellow prisoners. We shared the same beds, same foods, and same difficulties. We suffered no physical punishment such as torture and beatings. Three weeks after I arrived at the prison camp the Russians moved into the country and forced the Bulgarians to sign peace terms. We were freed and immediately sent across the border."

Blechhammer, Germany, was the target for the 15th Air Force bombers on August 27. After escorting the bombers over the target the 332nd attacked an enemy airfield while en route to the base. The enemy was caught by complete surprise and twenty-two planes were destroyed on the ground. On the mission Lieut. Emile C. Clifton, a member of the 99th Squadron, was forced to bail out of his plane over Yugoslavia when it developed engine trouble. However, he later returned to the base.

Captain Alfonso Davis of Omaha, Nebraska, led the 332nd in an attack on an enemy airfield at Grozwarden, Romania, on August 30. The 332nd was credited with eighty-three enemy aircraft destroyed on the ground. These planes had been evacuated previously from other enemy fields because of the rapid advance of the Russians. Captain Davis, happy because of his success, said, "They were parked like sitting ducks and all we had to do was line up our sights and shoot." Lieut. Roger Romine remarked, "When we went over the airport we looked like a cloud of grasshoppers swarming over a field of ripened wheat."

On August 31 the 332nd escorted B-17s of the 5th Bomb Wing to Bucharest, Romania. The mission was to evacuate American pilots and crewmen who had been shot down. This mission was particularly risky because the enemy still held the heavily defended territory. However, the mission was carried out with great success.

[108]

The flight leaders of a combat unit play a very important part in making a mission successful. The amount of confidence the men have in their leaders often determines the outcome of a battle or mission. On this mission to Bucharest on August 31, the 332nd was led by such a man as Lieut. Lawrence B. Jefferson of Grand Rapids, Michigan. "Bernie," as he was known by his comrades, had gained national fame before volunteering for pilot training. While attending Northwestern University he won recognition as a football star. When the war started this broad shouldered, unassuming lad volunteered for cadet training and was sent to Tuskegee Army Air Field. After gaining his wings he joined the 332nd Fighter Group and was sent overseas with the Group in January, 1944. Though never a colorful nor eager pilot Bernie's stability under pressure made him a valuable man to the Group.

Wherever German armies fought, Allied airmen carried the battle to them. On September 1 the 332nd was over Piteste, Romania. The next day it flew missions to Belgrade and Neskrs, Yugoslavia. Four days later one flight of the Group attacked a bridge south of Budapest, Hungary, while another flight escorted bombers to Romania. On September 8 the 332nd had another big day. It was credited with thirty-six of a total of seventy-six aircraft destroyed on airdromes in Yugoslavia by the 15th Air Force.

The 332nd took time out from combat on September 10 to reward four of its outstanding pilots. The four heroes were led to the runway by a parade of Group members. Here the four heroes were called to the front by the Group's adjutant to receive decorations for bravery in combat. The first to be decorated was Colonel Benjamin O. Davis, Jr. It was an extra special occasion for him because the decorating officer was his father, General Benjamin O. Davis. As the proud father stood before his son one sensed the personal delight that the occasion meant for him. He paused a while as if he was to shake hands with the hero and then as a General and a proud father remarked: "I am very proud of you." Shortly afterwards the citation was read.

"Benjamin O. Davis Jr., Colonel, Air Corps.,

For: Extraordinary achievement—in an aerial flight as pilot of a P-47 type aircraft, led his Group on a penetration escort attack on industrial targets in the Munich area June 9, 1944. The bomber formation was attacked by more than 100 enemy fighters near Udine, Italy. Faced with the problem of protecting the large bomber formation with the comparatively few fighters under his control, Colonel Davis so skillfully disposed his Squadron that in spite of the large number of enemy fighters, the bomber formation suffered only a few losses."

Captain Joseph D. Elsberry of 114 West Washington Boulevard, Langston, Oklahoma, was the next pilot to be decorated. His citation read: "For extraordinary achievement in aerial flight against the enemy in the North African and Mediterranean Theatres of operations, Captain Elsberry consistently aided in the success of combat operations. Against heavy opposition from both aggressive and persistent fighter aircraft and intense, heavy, and accurate enemy anti-aircraft fire, he has battled his way to his targets, defeating the enemy in the air, and destroying his vital installations on the ground. Through severe and adverse weather condition over treacherous mountain territory, he continuously surmounted overwhelming obstacles for successful completion of his assigned mission to attack and destroy the enemy."

The third hero decorated was 1st Lieut. Clarence D. Lester of Chicago, Illinois. His citation read: "On July 18, 1944, as a pilot of a P-51 type aircraft, Lieut. Lester participated in an escort mission for heavy bombers attack on enemy installations in Germany. En route to the target, the bomber formation was attacked by approximately 300 enemy aircraft, but despite the superiority in numbers of hostile ships, Lieut. Lester immediately engaged the hostile force in the ensuing engagement, displaying outstanding aggressiveness and combat proficiency. With complete disregard for his personal safety, he destroyed three enemy fighters, thus materially aiding in preventing the enemy from making concentrated attacks on the bombers."

The last to be decorated was Lieut. Jack D. Holsclaw of 2301 West College Avenue, Spokane, Washington. "On July 15, 1944, in an aerial flight as pilot of a P-51 type aircraft, Lieut. Holsclaw led his flight as escort to heavy bombers attacking enemy installations in Germany. Despite severe and adverse weather conditions, he brought his flight through to engage an enemy force of approximately 300 enemy fighters. With complete disregard for his personal safety, Lieut. Holsclaw with an outstanding display of aggressiveness and combat proficiency, destroyed two enemy fighters and forced the remainder to break off their organized attacks."

After the ceremony the decorated pilots were congratulated by several high officials of the Air Force. Among those present to congratulate the heroes were Lieut. General Ira C. Eaker, Commanding General of the Mediterranean Allied Air Force; Major General Nathan P. Twining, Commanding General of the 15th Air Force; and Brigadier General Dean C. Strother, Commanding General of the 15th Air Force Fighter Command.

The Legion of Merit was presented Colonel Davis by Lieut. General Eaker a week later. This citation created by Congress on July 20, 1942, is "Awarded to personnel of the Army of the United States and of the Armed Forces of friendly foreign nations, who have distinguished themselves by exceptionally meritorious conduct in the performance of outstanding services."

In September, 1944, news reached the 332nd Fighter Group that the Germans were perfecting a jet plane that was capable of flying much faster than the conventional planes. On September 12, 1944, Captain Edward Thomas of Chicago, Illinois, noted in his diary: "All Bomber Wings bombed airdromes and aircraft factories in the Munich area. We escorted the B-17 Wing and hit targets at Lechfeld, Germany. Reports say that the new German jet propelled plane can climb vertically and has a level flight speed in excess of 500 M.P.H."

Heavy bombers escorted by the 332nd struck Blechhammer, 150 miles east of Berlin, on September 13. Over the target Lieut. Wilbur F. Long's plane was hit by flak. His canopy was destroyed and his cooling system was severely damaged. Long was forced to crash land in Hungary. Upon landing he was captured by a group of civilians and turned over to the Germans.

The 332nd suffered another loss on September 22, when Flight Officer Leonard R. Willette of Belleville, New Jersey, was shot down while on a mission to Blechhammer, Germany. The adversities, however, did not stop the Group from striking targets in the various parts of Europe. On September 23 it was over Brux. The next day it struck targets in Blechhammer. The following day it was on escort to Regensburg. The Germans fought desperately to stave off defeat, but the continuous, around-the-clock attacks by the Allied Air Force had telling effect on the German war machine.

CHAPTER XVI

THE BATTLE OF GREECE

In the latter part of September, 1944, the weather in Italy was very bad. In fact, the weather was so bad that the whole 15th Air Force was grounded. For eight days a steady downpour kept the Allied Air Forces in Italy on the ground. But in some respect it gave the battle-tired pilots the much needed rest they had so valiantly earned.

In the meantime the German control in the Balkans was collapsing under the pressure of the Russian drive. The rapid sweep of the Russians through southeastern Romania threatened the Nazi control of the Balkans. Alarmed over their failure to halt the Russian drive, the Germans began evacuating several garrisons.

Near the end of September British forces invaded Greece which also was in the process of being evacuated by the Germans. A week later, on October 4, the weather broke in Italy and the 15th Air Force was sent into action against German Forces in Greece. The 332nd Fighter Group as a component of the 15th Air Force was assigned to strike enemy airfields in and around Athens which were threatening the British campaign.

Captain Erwin Lawrence led the Group on a mission to Greece on October 4, to knock out an enemy airfield. Just before reaching the target area each of the four Squadrons that comprised the Group was assigned different targets. These targets were enemy airfields at Eleusis, Totoi, Kolamoi, and Megara.

After the Group had split up to attack the different targets Captain Lawrence instructed Captain Edward Thomas, the leader of the second element of the 99th, that upon arrival over the target he was to furnish cover for the attacking flight.

Immediately upon reaching the enemy field Captain Lawrence fell into a dive with his flight following in string formation at close intervals. But the Germans were prepared for the attack and opened up with all their guns. Just as Captain Lawrence was about to pull out of his dive his ship was hit by a barrage of machine gun fire. Shortly afterwards the ship spun into the ground. Captain Thomas then took command of the squadron and continued the attack until the field was a mass of wreckage. Meantime Captain Freddie Hutchins of Donaldsonville, Georgia, a member of one of the other flights, had been knocked out of the sky at Megara. Freddie, a tall, round faced, jovial lad, related: "We were just approaching the target and I was flying with Lieut. Wilson on his first mission. As we approached the target run I told Wilson to start his run. However, it being Wilson's first mission, he became excited and was slow in opening up his plane. This retarded my run and cut down my speed. As I pulled up off the target I was hit by a volley of flak. I looked to my right and saw that my right wing tip was torn off completely. Looking back I noticed my tail assembly was practically shot apart. At this time flak was hitting my ship pretty consistently. I scooted down into my seat to get protection of the armored plates, but just at this time a volley of flak burst through the floor of my plane and struck my leg.

"I called Captain Dudley Watson, our flight leader, and told him that my plane had been damaged badly and that I couldn't stay up long. At the same time by some miracle I continued to gain altitude. I headed for friendly territory or rather a clear spot.

"I managed to clear a mountain peak by a few inches and then my plane began to lose altitude. I was now headed for some trees in a valley. I had very little control, but managed to miss the trees and crash landed into a small opening.

"I was knocked unconscious by the shock of the crash. When I came to, I found myself sitting at my controls with the engine of my plane lying several hundred feet away. My goggles were smashed on my forehead. My head was aching and my legs felt like they were broken. However, after examining my legs I found that they were all right except a deep flak wound on my left leg.

"I was pulled out of my ship by some Greeks who arrived at my plane shortly after it crashed. I walked a few steps, then passed out. Some men raised me up and began to walk me around. Then they put me on a donkey and walked the donkey around in a circle. They did this to restore my respiration. However, my back hurt me so badly I begged them to stop. I was then carried to a doctor who rubbed my back with some home made olive oil, strapped me up and put me to bed. The fleas had a wonderful time off me that night. The next day I decided I couldn't live through another such night so I made plans to leave though I was still in pain. I was taken into the city. There I gained transportation back to the base."

Meanwhile Lieut. Kenneth Williams had also run into trouble on the mission. While strafing an enemy airfield his plane was hit. He managed to gain sufficient altitude to bail out of his ship safely, but only to find his canopy was damaged and wouldn't open. He made a forced landing but was captured and taken to prison at an airfield. Later he was taken to the Luftwaffe headquarters in Athens and interrogated. Here he was joined by two more of his friends, Lieut. Joseph Lewis and Lieut. Carroll S. Woods, who were shot down two days after he went down.

"Six days after I was shot down the three of us, a British pilot, and British navigator, were placed aboard an evacuation train with a company of German soldiers. We traveled two weeks before arriving in Skopia, Yugoslavia. On the train I noticed the German soldiers were arrogant. They believed that a new weapon they had would change the tide of the war.

"At Skopia we learned that the Russians had cut the rails to the north. We were placed on a Ju-52 and flown to northern Yugoslavia. We were held at a local prison to await a train to Budapest, Hungary.

"The next morning we boarded a fast express to Budapest.

At Budapest we were placed in solitary confinement for five days. During the time we were in solitary confinement the Russians attacked Budapest. Several bombs struck near the jail damaging it considerably, breaking windows and shaking the building.

"On the fifth day we were sent to Frankfort on the Main. We stayed here five days then were carried to Wetzlar, a city about seventy miles from Frankfort. This was the first prison camp where we were allowed a little freedom and received Red Cross parcels. We stayed here three days; then on November 28, 1944, were sent to a permanent prison camp at Baleric, Germany. We hiked about one hundred miles to Spremberg before boarding a train. We ended up in Moosburg. This camp was overcrowded because the Germans were attempting to crowd prisoners from all the surrounding camps into this one camp. We were finally liberated on April 29, 1945 by the 3rd Army."

The mission to Athens on October 4 was not altogether unsuccessful. Lieuts. George R. Rhodes of Brooklyn, New York, George Gray of Welch, West Virginia, Shelby E. Westbrook of Toledo, Ohio, and Captain Edward Thomas of Chicago, Illinois, scored victories. Captain Henry B. Perry of Thomasville, Georgia, and Lieut. Milton Hayes of Los Angeles, California, were jointly credited with a victory. Captain Samuel Curtis's plane was damaged by flak, but he was able to nurse it back to the base and land safely.

On October 6 the 332nd returned to the Athens area to complete its assignment. The success of the mission can best be told by the citation of the late Captain Edward Thomas who was awarded the Distinguished Flying Cross by the War Department. The citation reads:

"Edward M. Thomas, 1st Lieut. Air Corps, 99th Fighter Squadron, 332nd Fighter Group.

"For extraordinary achievement in aerial flight P-51 type Aircraft in the Mediterranean theatre of operation. Lieut. Thomas' outstanding courage, aggressiveness and leadership enabled the formation to inflict damage upon a heavily defended airdrome in Athens, Greece. On October 6, 1944, Lieut. Thomas flew as a flight leader in a formation of fourteen (14) aircraft assigned to strafe the heavily defended Totoi Airdrome. Upon arrival in the target area Lieut. Thomas observed the position of the airdrome and the surrounding terrain. Upon approach of the formation towards the airfield. Lieut. Thomas' aircraft was hit by flak. Disregarding all thought of personal safety, Lieut. Thomas courageously pressed his attack to deck level and destroyed two (2) enemy aircraft and damaged another. Due to his exact judgement, skill and aggressiveness, a total of eleven (11) enemy aircraft was destroyed or damaged without loss to any aircraft of his section. Flying over treacherous, mountainous terrain, under adverse weather condition and against severe enemy opposition, Lieut. Thomas flew eighty-one (81) hazardous combat missions for a total of two hundred and fifty (250) combat hours. His outstanding courage, judgement, unquestionable devotion to duty and professional skill have reflected great credit upon himself and the Armed Forces of the United States of America."

Although the mission was successfully carried out, the Group lost two members, Lieuts. Carroll S. Woods and Joe Lewis. Both were shot down by flak bursts and were taken as prisoners by the Germans. They were held as prisoners at Moosburg, Germany, until General Patton's 3rd Army released all prisoners at the camp on April 29, 1945.

The Athens area was attacked by the 332nd for the third time on October 7. On this mission Lieut. Andrew D. Marshall of Bristol, Virginia, was forced to crash land his plane when it developed engine trouble while flying over the target area. Fortunately, however, he landed among some partisan Greeks who hid him from the Germans.

A week later, on October 14, after the British forces had consolidated the territory they had taken from the Germans, Marshall, astride a white horse at the head of a procession of several hundred peasants, rode from the hills of Megara into town. Here he received transportation back to the 332nd base. But fate was against Marshall. In December, 1944, he failed to return from a mission to Germany.

CHAPTER XVII

THE BALKAN CAMPAIGN

While the British were driving the Germans out of Greece other Allied forces were charging hard against the Germans in the Balkans. In Yugoslavia an army of partisans under Marshal Tito was driving toward the Danube to meet the swift moving Russians. In Albania and Czechoslovakia small specialized forces were harassing the Germans.

Meantime the Russians had met with great success. Russia's northern armies had repulsed German counter attacks in the Baltic, along the border of East Prussia, around Warsaw and Krakow. On August 20 an offensive launched from Jassay and Bessaralin had forced the Romanian government to turn against the Germans and their Ally, Hungary, on August 23. It also had compelled the Bulgarian government to break relations with Germany and sign an armistice on October 28.

The success of Russian troops in the Balkans deprived Germany of all her Allies except Hungary and opened the southern flank of Germany to the threat of an invasion through Hungary, Austria, and Czechoslovakia. The continued drive by the Russian armies through Romania pushed west to the Iron Gate leading into Yugoslavia, where for more than a year partisan Guerrillas under Marshal Tito had kept 125,000 enemy troops occupied. With the British advancing in Greece, the Germans could only hope to retain control of escape routes through Yugoslovia.

The 332nd Fighter Group also played its part in the Balkan campaign. It escorted bombers of the 15th Air Force to strike targets throughout the Balkans. It aided partisan forces in Yugoslavia and Czechoslovakia and dive bombed and strafed

Nazi strong points that hindered the advance of the Russian Army.

On October 7, 1944, the 332nd strafed targets in Yugoslavia which were causing the partisan forces under Marshal Tito considerable trouble. While strafing, Lieut. Robert H. Wiggins' plane was damaged by a flak burst. Wiggins attempted to fly his ship back to the base, but while en route was forced to land on the Isle of Vis.

After repairing his ship Wiggins took off again for his base. En route he picked up a crippled C-47 and escorted it to the Foggia area. Then, after seeing the bomber land safely, he struck out for home. Somehow he wandered off course and crashed into the Adriatic Sea. Later his body was recovered and buried in the American Cemetery in Bari, Italy.

On October 11 the 332nd, led by Lieut. George E. Gray of Welch, West Virginia, escorted bombers to Hungary. En route to the base the Group attacked an enemy airfield and destroyed seventeen Nazi aircraft on the ground. The Group also destroyed a locomotive and several oil tankers. The next day the 332nd lost Lieut. Walter L. McCreary of San Antonio, Texas. While on an escort mission to Hungary his plane was hit by a flak burst. He bailed out of his ship in the Lake Balaton area. Upon hitting the ground, he was pounced upon by a mob of angry civilians. Fortunately, he was rescued by a group of German soldiers who broke up the mob and led McCreary off to prison.

As the Germans retreated before the Russian Army, McCreary was moved from prison to prison. He finally ended up in Moosburg, Germany, where he was held a prisoner until the American 3rd Army captured the city and released all the prisoners.

Nine enemy aircraft were shot down and twenty-six were destroyed, on the ground during an attack on Blechhammer, Germany, by the 332nd on October 12, 1944. Lieut. Lee Archer was top scorer with three victories, Captain Wendell Pruitt was credited with two victories, and Captain Milton R. Brooks was credited with one enemy aircraft. Lieuts. William W. Green, Luther H. Smith Jr., and Roger Romine also were credited with a victory each.

One Saturday afternoon I ventured down to the Operation office at Tuskegee to talk with Captain Baugh and Lee Archer. Sometime during the course of our conversation we began to talk about Wendell Pruitt, who had been killed a short time before in a plane accident near the field. This led to the mission of October 12, on which Archer and Pruitt scored victories. This is how Archer related what happened on that day.

"The mission was bomber escort to Blechhammer, Germany. On this mission the 302nd was the low squadron and we flew to the extreme right of the other squadrons. We had just crossed Lake Balaton when I spied a group of enemy aircraft at two o'clock on the tree top. These planes were just beginning to take off from an enemy airfield.

"I called in the bandits and Pruitt was the first to pick up my message. He peeled off from the formation, rolled his plane over, and dived for the enemy aircraft. I followed close behind him as he made two passes at a H. E. 111.

"A short while later I looked down and saw about twelve enemy ships taking off on the runway. They seemed to have been escort planes for the H.E. 111 that was just beginning to take off from the runway. I called in that twelve enemy aircraft were taking off below. Somehow I didn't receive any answer from the rest of the Group. I later learned that Lieut. L. H. Smith and Lieut. William Green had engaged the enemy ships and were successful in shooting two of them down.

"In the meantime Pruitt made a third pass at the enemy plane and as he pulled up I noticed the enemy plane smoking. I followed Pruitt's victim and gave him a long burst and the ship disintegrated in the air. However, I couldn't claim this victory because Pruitt had damaged the plane so badly that it was only a matter of seconds before it would have spun into the ground.

"Just after we had destroyed our first plane Pruitt noticed

the formation of enemy planes coming directly toward us. Instead of avoiding them Pruitt flew directly into the formation with his guns blazing away.

"As we passed through the formation the planes scattered. We were now flying side by side with the enemy planes going in the opposite direction.

"We made a tight turn and fell in behind three enemy aircraft. After getting within shooting distance I fired a couple of short bursts at one of the planes. My fire was accurate and I tore off the wing of the plane. It tumbled down to earth. Then I slid my plane down below Pruitt's plane which was now on the tail of a second plane. However, before I could fire, Pruitt's shots hit the target. The plane burst into flame.

"At this time a ME-109 came in from the left and slid in behind Pruitt who was now on the tail of a third enemy plane. I immediately pulled up behind him and gave a few short bursts, the plane exploded, throwing the pilot out of the cockpit and then fell to the ground.

"Pruitt was still chasing the plane he had lined up. However, on his third burst his guns jammed. As I pulled up beside him I could see him fiddling with his controls trying to start his guns. Seeing that Pruitt wasn't getting any results I told him to move over and let a man shoot who could shoot. He pulled over and I eased my plane into his position. I gave the enemy plane a long burst. Then the ME-109 went into a dive for a runway that I observed below. Seemingly, he had decided to land. I gave him another long burst and he crashed on the runway. The German ground crew opened up with all their guns. Lights were blinking at me from all directions. For a few seconds I had to dodge flak and small arm fire that burst all around my ship. But I was lucky and managed to wiggle out."

One Sunday afternoon a group of us held a little "Bull session" in Lieut. William Thomas' room down at Tuskegee. Thomas, a slender Californian, loved music. He had records of most of the outstanding orchestras and a selection of classical records that ranked among the best on the post. Naturally, this was an ideal place to lounge around and pass away Sundays which were usually dull and unexciting. Anyway, the conversation got around to experiences in combat.

I asked Thomas if he had known Westmoreland. "Yes, Westmoreland was one of my best friends," said Thomas. "He was a very likable fellow, rather quiet and unassuming. You know, he was the nephew of Walter White, Secretary of the N. A. A. C. P.

"Anyway, a few weeks before I arrived in Naples he had bailed out of a P-39 Aerocobra and hurt his leg. When I arrived overseas he was using a crutch to get around. But he recovered and resumed flying.

"On October 12, 1944, the Group was assigned to escort heavy and medium bombers to Blechhammer, about 125 miles from Berlin. Before we took off we agreed we would strike anything we saw on the way back to the base.

"During the mission Dubois Ross had trouble with his plane so Lieut. Lee Archer had to follow Ross until his plane straightened out. Near Lake Balaton we spotted an enemy airfield and we decided to strafe it. Before this, however, we made passes at a shipping port and hit a ship. Anyway on the enemy airfield there was a high building. As we made our run in to attack the field we noticed small lights blinking at us, so we knew the enemy was firing on us from the building.

"When the time came for me to make my run I headed towards the building with all my guns blazing away. As I pulled up I noticed I was almost out of ammunition, so I decided to take pictures of the action. I decided to circle the field and make my run in from the entrance pattern. As I reached the entrance point I noticed one of our ships going into the field with all of its guns blazing away at the building. As the ship pulled up I noticed smoke coming from it. Then the plane rocked and headed into the field. I watched the plane as it hit the field, skipped a good distance, and turned over on its back, tearing off its wings.

"After making my second pass I pulled up and circled

[123]

over the wrecked plane, but I didn't see Westmoreland get out of the plane. Then I rejoined my formation.

"Immediately after rejoining the formation Captain Melvin Jackson, our flight leader, decided to brave the enemy guns and go down to take pictures of the wreckage. He went down in spite of the heavy enemy machine gun fire and took pictures of the wreckage. Then he rejoined us and we returned to the base. The pictures were immediately developed, but they revealed nothing to give us hope that Westmoreland had come out of the accident all right."

While Captain Jackson's flight was attacking the enemy airfield another flight led by Captain Wendell Pruitt was strafing a railroad junction. They shot up box cars, locomotives, and buildings. Two pilots of the flight, Lieuts. Luther "Preacher" Smith and William W. "Chubby" Green, hit a large barn filled with explosives. The barn blew up so suddenly that the debris damaged the planes in flight.

When Lieut. Smith got to the border of Yugoslavia his coolant was running out of his plane so fast he was forced to bail out. Lieut. Green circled Smith as he floated down. Immediately upon landing Smith was taken to prison by the Nazis. He was released by the Allies at the end of the war and returned to the States.

Not long after Smith went down Green noticed the temperature of his gauge rising fast. He called his flight leader, but received no response. Captain Melvin Jackson later related that he heard Green say that he was headed for the emergency landing field on the Isle of Vis. However, before Green could reach the emergency field he was forced to bail out of his ship. He was picked up by a group of partisans and taken to a divisional headquarters of Marshal Tito's army. The following day he volunteered to help a British supply mission drop supplies to Tito's men scattered in various sections of the country.* Four

---

*At the end of the war Lieut. Green received the order of the Partisan Star III class. This award by the government of Yugoslavia was presented to Lieut. Green by Colonel Benjamin O. Davis Jr. in a colorful review ceremony at Godman Field, Kentucky.

days later some Russian pilots landed at the base where Green was staying and they agreed to fly Green back to his base in Naples.

While Green and Smith were having their troubles Lieut. Archer was also having trouble. Archer's plane had been hit in the propeller when he followed his last victim down too close to the enemy airfield. Captain Pruitt decided to escort him to the base. While flying over a high mountain range on the return to the base Archer's plane began to act up. He managed to keep his plane in the air and continued on to the Isle of Vis.

On landing, Captain Pruitt gassed up and shortly afterwards took off for his home base. Lieut. Archer immediately set about to replace the propeller of his ship with another he took from a junked plane. He returned to his home base the following day.

The 332nd was again sent to Blechhammer on October 14. On this mission Lieut. Ruall Bell was shot down ten miles northeast of Zagreb in Yugoslavia. During the battle he was wounded. He bailed out of his ship and on landing he was picked up by British soldiers and sent to an American hospital in Bari, Italy.

On the same day, Captain Alfonso Davis of Omaha, Nebraska, led an escort mission to Southeastern Germany to strike the Odestal Oil Works. During the attack Lieut. Robert J. Friend of Washington, D. C., strafed an oil barge, pouring 50 calibre bullets into its hull. The bullets found their mark and all of a sudden the barge belched a huge mushroom shaped flame just as Friend's ship reached her. The flames completely engulfed the diving plane. Luckily, Friend managed to pull his plane through the flames without damage.

Captain Armour McDaniel sprayed another barge and was also fortunate in clearing the deck just as a tremendous blast ripped the barge to pieces. The force of the blast was so great that all of McDaniel's wing guns were ripped out of his ship. In spite of the severe damage he was able to nurse his plane back to the base in Naples.

[125]

Colonel Davis led the 332nd on a mission to Austria on October 15, and the following day Captain Melvin Jackson led a mission to Upper Silesia. On October 20 the Group escorted bombers to Brux. Three days later it was over Regensburg and Yugoslavia. Most of these missions were uneventful, but on the mission to Yugoslavia the Group lost Lieut. Robert C. Chandler of Allegan, Michigan, and Shelby F. Westbrook of Toledo, Ohio. Both of these pilots were shot down by enemy ack-ack guns.

Throughout the last two months of 1944, the 15th Air Force, cooperating with the swiftly moving Russians, struck targets throughout the Balkans and Europe. On November 7, the 332nd escorted bombers to Southeastern Austria. En route to the base after completing its mission the Group flew high over a slight overcast. In the vicinity of Reuhenfels, Austria, Captain William Faulkner of Nashville, Tennessee, peeled off from his formation and headed straight downward.

Upon receiving the news that Faulkner had broken formation, the flight leader made a quick turn and at the same time ordered his men to watch for the missing pilot. They combed the area and went down as close to the ground as safety permitted, but no trace of Faulkner's ship could be found. The flight then assembled and continued its journey back to the base. No information as to what happened to Captain Faulkner was ever obtained. It is the belief of those who flew with Faulkner on the fatal mission that his oxygen tank failed him, that he had blacked out from the lack of oxygen, and crashed without regaining consciousness.

The 332nd added another victorious page to its record on November 16 as a result of the success of Captain Luke Weathers, a native of Memphis, Tennessee. After escorting bombers to the Munich area, Captain Weathers, together with Captain Melvin Jackson and Captain Louis Purnell, was detailed to escort a crippled bomber to its base. Over northern Italy eight enemy planes were sighted at 2 o'clock high. However, when first sighted they were too far off to be identified as enemy aircraft. As the planes approached they were recognized as ME-109s and preparations were made for the attack. Captain Weathers who was flying escort on the side of the approaching aircraft peeled off and met the enemy planes in a head on attack. When they got within shooting distance he opened fire. After a few bursts from his guns one of the enemy planes fell into a dive and began to split S down to earth. At this time Weathers began to notice little red balls sailing past his canopy. He glanced around in time to notice that a second enemy aircraft was on his tail and was blazing away, trying desperately to make the kill.

Meantime, Captain Jackson and Captain Purnell had noticed the enemy aircraft following Weathers. They fell in behind the enemy plane, but before they could open fire they were attacked from the rear by the remaining enemy planes. They were forced to go into a dive to avoid being shot down.

Instead of the enemy pilots pressing their attacks on Jackson and Purnell they decided to concentrate on Weathers. They circled him and closed in from all directions as their comrade followed close on Weathers' tail. This was the German "Wolf Pack" and with the battle in its favor it was determined to make the kill.

Though he was greatly outnumbered Weathers kept his composure. He refused to be shot down. Relating how he escaped being shot down, Weathers said: "It looked like they had me so I decided to follow the falling plane. I made a dive, came out of it and looked back. One plane was still on my tail. I was headed back towards Germany and I didn't want to go that way. I chopped my throttle and dropped my flaps to cut my speed quickly. The fellow overshot me and this left me on his tail. He was in range so I opened fire. A long burst and a few short bursts sent him tumbling to the ground."

In combat a man is respected if he has "guts" no matter where he is from, what his religious beliefs are, or the color of his skin. Captain Weathers experienced this in Naples, Italy. A pilot from another fighter group joined Captain Weathers' party one night while at a little club in Naples. In the conversation that followed the new acquaintance mentioned that he was a cousin of a former governor of Mississippi. He then stated that he had the utmost respect for members of the 332nd because some pilots of the Group had probably saved his life when he was being attacked by a group of German fighters. After hearing the incidents of the mission Captain Weathers decided that he himself was one of the members of the escort mission that had fought off the Germans.

Captain Weathers was given the keys to the city by the mayor of Memphis on June 25, 1945, on the occasion of the Seventh War Loan Drive. The *Commercial Appeal* and the *Press Seminary,* two of the leading newspapers of Memphis, Tennessee, carried Weathers' picture and his speech. This was an honor never before bestowed on a Negro by that city.

The victories by the 332nd on November 16 were not gained without a price. While taking off on the mission, planes flown by Lieuts. Roger Romine and William Hill collided. Romine was killed and Hill suffered severe facial and body burns as a result of a fire started by the collision. Lieut. Hill was pulled out of his ship and sent to an American hospital at Bari, Italy, where he recuperated.

On November 19 Lieut. Quitman Walker of Indianola, Mississippi, and Lieut. Robert B. Gaither of New Jersey were shot down while strafing in Hungary. Both pilots survived the experience of being shot down in enemy territory. Lieut. Gaither evaded the Nazis four days before he was captured. Then he was taken to Gyor where he joined six other airmen who also had been shot down. A few days later the prisoners were marched to a railroad station for shipment to Germany. At the station they were pounced upon by a mob of angry civilians and severely clubbed before the guards decided to come to their rescue. Bruised and bleeding, the prisoners were then placed on a train and shipped to Vienna. From Vienna they were sent to Germany where they were held until released by the Allied army at the end of the war.

The day after Walker and Gaither were shot down Lieut. Maceo A. Harris of Boston, Massachusetts, failed to return from a mission over Germany. This loss was followed by another seven days later when Lieut. Elton H. Nightengale failed to return from a mission to Southern Germany.

Lieut. Nightengale was flying as wingman for Captain Stanley Harris when he disappeared. Captain Harris, relating the mission, stated that they were flying above a heavy layer of clouds at approximately 30,000 feet. They broke into a small opening and saw the bombers they were assigned to protect, flying directly below. Upon spotting the bombers Captain Harris made a tight turn in order to place his flight in a position to go down to protect the bombers. In making the turn, however, he lost Nightengale. Realizing that he had lost his wingman, Captain Harris turned back to catch up with Nightengale. Meantime, Nightengale had turned back to join the flight. This placed Harris and Nightengale still traveling in opposite directions. By this time the clouds had closed in. This made it impossible for Harris to locate the missing plane. However, he was able to contact Nightengale by radio. He gave Nightengale his course and told him to strike out for the base. For a while they kept contact with each other, but later lost contact. Nightengale failed to return to the base and was never heard from again.

On December 2 Lieut. Cornelius Gould Jr. failed to return from a mission over Czechoslovakia. He became a prisoner of war and was held until the end of the war. Lieut. Andrew D. Marshall of Bristol, Virginia, and Lieut. Frederick Funderburg of Monticello, Georgia, failed to return from a mission on December 28. The next day while returning from a mission over Vienna, Austria, Lieut. Lewis W. Craig, a member of the 99th Squadron, was forced to bail out of his ship while flying over the Adriatic Sea. In the fall Craig dislocated his shoulder, but fortunately was rescued from drowning by some Italian civilians. He was placed on a British hospital ship and carried to an American hospital at Bari, Italy, where he was treated.

By the end of 1944 the Germans were practically without an ally. They had lost considerable ground in the east and had been pushed out of Russian teritory. The Balkan countries were practically lost, Finland had turned upon Germany, half of Poland had been liberated, and the assault on Warsaw was about to begin. Though far from defeated, Germany was definitely on the defensive.

CHAPTER XVIII

THE COLLAPSE OF GERMANY

By January, 1945, the effects of the Allied Air offensive against the Germans were becoming apparent. The Air Force had achieved remarkable success in depleting the enemy's oil reserves, disrupting his transportation and communication systems, and demoralizing his troops. The Nazis found it increasingly difficult to transport reserve troops and supplies from one front to another, and their armies, on all fronts, suffered from the lack of fuel for vehicles.

Although Germany's defeat seemed inevitable, the Allies were cautious of her inventive genius. During the fall and winter of 1944 the Allied Army Intelligence staff reported that the Germans were making considerable progress in the development of jet planes. Increasing numbers of these heavily armed jets were seen in the sky, but they were neither sufficiently numerous nor sufficiently aggressive to constitute a major threat. However, reports of the speed and maneuverability of these new jets caused Allied Commanders to make immediate plans for the destruction of their factories. They knew that technically the jet was far ahead of any aircraft the Allies had in action. They also realized that should Germany succeed in putting into the air a considerable number of these new planes they could exact heavy losses to the Allied bombers operating against her.

To delay the production of jet planes the Air Force decided upon an all out campaign against Nazi aerial production centers. Early in January Allied bombers and fighters were again sent out to strike enemy areas which were believed to be jet construction centers.

Meantime, while the war against German aircraft factories was in progress, other developments that would eventually spell finish for the German domination of Europe were in progress. The American and British Forces in the West were preparing for a swift campaign across the Rhine and into Germany. In the east the Russians were forging ahead in the Balkans. The great armies of Russia along the center of their thousand mile front were reorganizing for a final lunge. In the southern sectors of the Russian line, Russian armies were driving into Hungary and Austria, seeking to outflank Germany from the south in one of the greatest encircling operations in military history.

At the beginning of the new year the Russian campaign in the east seemed distant and somewhat confused. But her new offensive which started on January 12, 1945, was one of phenomenal success. In three weeks the Russians drove 275 miles from Warsaw, Poland, to Frankfurt on the Oder.

The 15th Air Force was also doing its part in the offensive to crush Germany. It operated against German jet production centers, hit targets in central and Southern Germany, and dive bombed and strafed enemy troops and supplies in all sectors. It struck targets in Czechoslovakia, Yugoslavia, Hungary, Austria, and Poland.

Pilots of the 332nd Fighter Group shared with their comrades of the 15th Air Force in bringing the war in Europe to an end. Wherever the 15th Air Force bombers flew the 332nd acted as escort. They were over Vienna one day, over Budapest the next day. They struck targets in Munich and battered German airmen over Berlin. They went on fighter sweeps into Poland and blasted Nazi supply lines and communication centers in Yugoslavia.

Throughout the months of January and February, 1945, the 332nd was kept continuously busy. On February 1 it escorted bombers to Yugoslavia. This mission was led by Captain Armour C. McDaniel of Martinsville, Virginia. However, no enemy aircraft were encountered during the mission.

Major George "Spanky" Roberts led a strafing mission to the Munich area on the same day. On this mission the 332nd scored its first aerial victory of the new year when Lieut. William S. Price of Topeka, Kansas, shot down a German ME-109. The Group was also credited with destroying five enemy aircraft on the ground, seven locomotives, five box cars, and one flat car. The victorious pilots were Lieuts. Henry R. Peoples of St. Louis, Missouri, three locomotives; Jimmie D. Wheeler of Roseville, Michigan, one locomotive; Roscoe C. Browne of New York City, one locomotive; Harry T. Stewart of Corona, Illinois, one Ju-52 transport plane destroyed on the ground; Lionel Bonan of Pascagoula, Mississippi, one FW-190 destroyed on the ground; John W. Davis, Kansas City, Kansas, five box cars and one flat car; F/O James Fischer of Stoughton, Massachusetts, one locomotive; F/O Wyrian T. Schell of Brooklyn, New York, one locomotive.

The 332nd escorted heavy and medium bombers to Vienna and Moosbierbaum on February 8. The next day it escorted bombers to Vienna to destroy a huge ordnance depot. On February 12 Colonel Davis led a mission to Vienna. The success of the mission is best told by Captain Louis R. Purnell, a youthful Maryland lad, who had entered combat with the original 99th Squadron. "It was a beautiful sight. Looking off the corner of my left wing I saw a terrific explosion and then clouds of smoke rose high. The explosion flames must have risen at least two hundred feet. The sight made me think of the old days over Ploesti targets."

On February 13 and 14 the 332nd escorted bombers to Vienna to knock out a central repair depot. Nürnberg, Germany, was attacked by the Group on February 17. The next day it returned to Vienna. A marshalling yard in Brenner, Germany, was the target on February 20. Two days later the Group escorted bombers to the Munich area. It aided in knocking out a marshalling yard in Gmunden, Austria, on the 23rd, and returned to the Munich area on the 25th.

During the mission of February 25 the 332nd lost two of its members, Lieuts. George Iles and Wendell W. Hockaday. While strafing in the Munich area, Iles' ship was knocked out of the sky by enemy ack-ack guns. He was taken to prison and held until released by the American Third Army at the end of the war. Lieut. Hockaday allowed the wing of his ship to hit a locomotive while strafing. He managed to pull his ship up after it had been severely damaged. A little later he was forced to bail out over the Alps when his ship began to falter. He was never seen or heard of again. It is the belief of many of his friends that he was killed when he hit the rocky mountains.

The day-to-day experiences of a fighter group are as varied as life itself. Unexpected things happen each day. The 332nd flew missions to Merano, Italy, on March 1. On March 7, 1945, the Group lost Flight Officer Thomas Hawkins when his plane crashed on the runway while taking off on a mission. A week later, March 14, Lieut. Samuel Washington was shot down over Vienna while strafing a freight train. A flak burst damaged his fuel line and hydraulic system. A second burst severely damaged his instrument panel. Despite the damages, he stuck with his crippled plane and nursed it into friendly territory in Yugoslavia. He landed in a field and was later picked up by a British Liaison pilot and carried to Zagreb where he stayed four days before returning to his base.

Another member of the 332nd, Lieut. Harold Brown, also went down the same day. A locomotive that he had just strafed blew up under his plane. He was forced to bail out. Twenty minutes after hitting the ground he was picked up by some civilian policemen and turned over to the Germans. He was held as a prisoner of war until released at the end of the war by Allied troops.

The 332nd escorted bombers to Linz, Austria, on March 20, 1945. Over the target Lieut. Newman C. Golden's plane developed engine trouble which forced him to bail out fifty miles west of the target area. He was captured and held as a prisoner by the Germans. Three days later Lieut. Lincoln Hudson's plane was hit by flak burst while on a mission to Ruhland, seventy-five miles south of Berlin. He attempted to fly to the Russian line but en route his engine failed. He landed in Czechoslovakia. Lieut. Rapier, Hudson's escort, circled the helpless pilot until he landed safely, then returned to the base.

On March 24 Colonel Davis led the 332nd on one of the longest missions (1600 miles) ever attempted by the 15th Air Force. The pilots were briefed to bomb the Daimler Benz Tank Works in Berlin. However, the mission was actually designed as a diversionary effort to draw off German fighters based in Central Germany which might otherwise have been committed against the airborne landings north of the Ruhr.

It was planned that the 332nd would relieve a P-38 Fighter Group at 11 o'clock over Brux and carry the bombers to the outskirts of Berlin. At this time the 332nd was to be relieved by another P-51 group which would escort the bombers over the target. Upon the arrival at the point where it was to be relieved, the 332nd was instructed to continue over the target because the relief group was late.

Just before reaching the target, Colonel Davis' plane developed engine trouble which forced him to turn back. Captain Armour McDaniel then took over the command. Over the target the 332nd encountered the new German jet planes for the first time. In the ensuing battle pilots of the Group destroyed three of the jets. Captain Roscoe Browne of New York City, Lieut. Earle R. Lane of Wickliffe, Ohio, and Flight Officer Charles V. Brantley of St. Louis, Missouri, were credited with the victories.

The mission, however, was not without losses. During the battle Lieuts. Ronald Reeves and Robert C. Robinson were shot down. Both pilots failed to return to the base and later were listed as missing in action. Captain Armour McDaniel, the group leader, was also shot down. He was captured by the Germans and held as a prisoner of war. Lieut. Leon W. Spears was forced to land in Russian held territory when his plane was severely damaged. A fifth member of the flight, Lieut. Hannibal Cox, was forced to hit the deck to keep from being shot down by an enemy aircraft.

Lieut. Jimmie Lanham, relating the mission, said: "I was

[135]

flying in the 'thin man's' (Colonel Davis) flight on the mission. I was an element leader and Whitney (Yenwith) was my wingman. McDaniel had blue flight. Colonel Davis' plane developed engine trouble just before we reached Berlin so he returned to the base and McDaniel took over the Group. After we were attacked by the jets I heard Schell (Wyrian) say, 'Mc-Daniel just got shot down.' Someone said, 'There he goes.' I heard Walter Manning say, 'Here's a whole bunch of them.' A jet came in at 90 degrees to attack the bombers. We made a 180 degree turn, but the jets went over the horizon before we could get to the attack point. There were about twenty-five enemy planes in the air."

Although heavy losses were sustained, the mission was successfully carried out. For successfully escorting the bombers the Group was awarded the Distinguished Unit Citation.

WAR DEPARTMENT
BUREAU OF PUBLIC RELATIONS
PRESS BRANCH

October 16, 1945

IMMEDIATE   RELEASE

332ND FIGHTER GROUP WINS
DISTINGUISHED UNIT CITATION

In the name of the President of the United States, as "public evidence of deserved honor and distinction," a Distinguished Unit Citation has been conferred upon the all-Negro 332nd Fighter Group for outstanding performance of duty in armed conflict with the enemy, the War Department announced today.

The citation reads as follows:

"On March 23, 1945, the group was assigned the mission of escorting heavy bombardment type aircraft attacking the vital Daimler-Benz tank assembly plant at Berlin, Germany. Realizing the strategic importance of the mission and fully cognizant of the amount of enemy resistance to be expected and the long range to be covered, the ground crews worked tirelessly and with enthusiasm to have their aircraft at the peak of mechanical condition to insure the success of the operation.

"On March 24, 1945, fifty-nine P-51 type aircraft were airborne and set course for the rendezvous with the bomber formation. Through superior navigation and maintenance of strict flight discipline the group formation reached the bomber formation at the designated time and place. Nearing the target approximately 25 enemy aircraft were encountered which included ME-252s which launched relentless attacks in a desperate effort to break up and destroy the bomber formation.

"Displaying outstanding courage, aggressiveness, and combat technique, the group immediately engaged the enemy formation in aerial combat. In the ensuing engagement that continued over the target area, the gallant pilots of the 332nd Fighter Group battled against the enemy fighters to prevent the breaking up of the bomber formation and thus jeopardizing the successful completion of this vitally important mission. Through their superior skill and determination, the group destroyed three enemy aircraft, probably destroyed three and damaged three. Among their claims were eight of the highly rated enemy jet-propelled aircraft with no losses sustained by the 332nd Fighter Group.

"Leaving the target area and en route to base after completion of their primary task, aircraft of the group conducted strafing attacks against enemy ground installation and transportation with outstanding success. By the conspicuous gallantry, professional skill, and determination of the pilots, together with the outstanding technical skill and devotion to duty of the ground personnel, the 332nd Fighter Group has reflected great credit on itself and the armed forces of the United States."

The 332nd scored one of its most outstanding victories on Saturday, March 31, 1945. While on a strafing mission near Linz, Austria, it encountered a flight of enemy aircraft. In a wild dog fight the Group was successful in shooting down thirteen of the enemy planes without losing a plane. The victorious pilots were:

Major William A. Campbell, Tuskegee, Alabama, 1 ME-109
Lieut. Robert W. Williams, Ottumwa, Iowa, 2 FW-190s
Lieut. Bertram W. Wilson, Brooklyn, New York, 1 FW-190
Lieut. Daniel L. Rich, Rutherford, New Jersy, 1 ME-109
Lieut. Rual W. Bell, Portland, Oregon, 1 FW-190
Lieut. Thomas P. Braswell, Buford, Georgia, 1 FW-190
Lieut. John W. Davis, Kansas City, Kansas, 1 ME-109
Lieut. James L. Hall Jr., Washington, D. C., 1 ME-109
Lieut. Hugh J. White, St. Louis, Missouri, 1 ME-109
Lieut. Roscoe C. Browne, New York City, 1 FW-190
Lieut. Earle R. Lane, Wickliffe, Ohio, 1 ME-109
Flight Officer John H. Lyle, Chicago, Illinois, 1 FW-190

Lieut. Robert Williams, who was credited with two victories, related: "I dived into a group of enemy aircraft. After getting on the tail of one of the enemy planes I gave him a few short bursts. My fire hit the mark and the enemy plane fell off and tumbled to the ground. On pulling away from my victim I found another enemy plane on my tail. To evade his guns I made a steep turn. Just as I had turned another enemy plane shot across the nose of my plane. Immediately, I began firing on him. The plane went into a steep dive and later crashed."

The next day, April 1, the 332nd led by Captain Walter H. Downs of Oakland, California, provided escort penetration, target cover, and withdrawal for B-24s of the 47th Bomb Wing to St. Polten marshalling yard. It encountered a group of enemy aircraft near Wels, Austria, and destroyed twelve more planes. This brought the total victories for two days of fighting to twenty-five enemy planes destroyed in the air.

The top scorer of the day was Lieut. Harry T. Stewart Jr. of Corona, Long Island, who was credited with three victories. The other victories were credited as follows: Captain Charles White, Oakland, California, 2 aircraft; Lieuts. Earl Carey, St. Louis, Missouri, 2 aircraft; John E. Edwards, Steubenville, Ohio,

[138]

2 aircraft; Harold Morris, Portland, Oregon, 1 aircraft; Walter Manning, 1 aircraft; Flight Officer James Fischer, Stoughton, Massachusetts, 1 aircraft.

Perhaps the luckiest pilot on the mission was Flight Officer Fischer. In fact, Fischer felt that he was one of the luckiest pilots in the world. The story he related seems to substantiate this fact. This is his story of the mission on April 1, 1945:

"Colonel Davis flew with our Squadron, the 301st, on this mission. On the way to the target he told us that on our return from the mission we were free to hunt trouble. After fulfilling our mission the 301st broke away from the rest of the Group and flew straight down the Danube river. We found nothing of interest in the Danube area, but when we got to Linz we met a great deal of flak. Frankly, we were looking for enemy barges on the river, but instead sighted enemy planes.

Our leader, Lieut. Charles White, called in the enemy aircraft. However, just at this time I began having trouble. When I tried to release my wing tanks I found that they were stuck. By the time I was able to release them the fight was on. At this time the Jerries were attacking us from the rear. I wheeled my plane around and ploughed through the enemy formation and in spite of the concentration of enemy fire I didn't get hit. But after I had passed through the formation I found myself somewhat alone. So I immediately turned and re-joined my formation.

"In the distance I saw an enemy aircraft smoking and, looking downward, I got a glance at one of our planes crashing to the ground. Above me I saw smoke streaming from another P-51 as it made a steep turn. A FW-190 was directly behind it, firing away with all of its guns.

"I pulled up behind the Focke-Wulf that was firing on the smoking plane. I gave him several bursts from my guns. After I made several direct hits on the enemy ship it made a dive for the ground. I followed him down, but as I approached the ground I met a volley of fire from the enemy ground crew. I was hit several times. My rudder and canopy were damaged.

By some miracle my ship managed to stay in the air. A few seconds later I dropped down behind a hill and out of range of the enemy ground force. I checked my plane and found that my rudder cable was badly damaged. I called my leader and told him that my plane was damaged so badly that I was heading for Russian held territory. I was at this time about ten or fifteen miles from Vienna.

"I flew to Vienna and turned south with the idea of landing in Yugoslavia. I started climbing about this time to get above the Alps. As I crossed a small factory town the enemy opened up with their 88's. They tore a hole in my wing. My plane began to lose gas and a little later my engine quit. I switched tanks and the engine caught up. I was left with about 55 gallons of gasoline on the north side of the Alps. My engine had only about one-third of its power, because I had run it at top speed too long.

"I called Big Friend, our distress code call, but received no answer. Finally, after several calls, a British Commando radio emergency station picked me up and steered me to Zagreb. Just as I got over the coast line my ship gave out of gas. I was flying at 14,000 feet and the field was in sight. I glided my plane toward the field. Realizing that I had no rudder, I decided it was too risky to attempt a landing. I decided to jump. I was afraid to turn my plane over, so I crawled over the side of my ship and fell out. In my fall I hit the damaged rudder and my plane fell into a spin. I pulled my chute cord as I fell out of my ship. When I opened my eyes I found myself upside down, floating down to earth with silk all over my head.

"When I landed a lot of Yugoslavian kids and grown-ups gathered around me. An L-5 observation plane came over a few minutes later and spotted me. A little later a jeep and ambulance arrived to take me to the emergency strip. I was put on a C-47 and sent back to Rametelli in time for supper.

"When I arrived at the field, I learned that the two pilots I saw in trouble during the dog fight were Lieut. Walter Manning and Flight Officer William Armstrong. They failed to return from the mission."

By the first of April, 1945, the German army was completely demoralized. It had suffered an unbroken series of major defeats. Beginning with the Battle of the Bulge on December 17, 1944, the Allied war machine inflicted upon the Germans a series of losses and defeats. In both the east and the west strong Allied forces were now operating in the homeland of Germany. The great industrial centers of Germany, the Ruhr, the Saar, and Silesia, were all lost to the enemy. Germany's remaining industries, dispersed over the central area of the country, could not possibly support her armies still attempting to fight. Communications were badly broken and no Nazi senior commander could be sure that his orders would reach the troops. Only on the nothern and southern flanks of the great western front were there armies of sufficient size to do more than delay Allied advances.

On March 31 General Eisenhower issued a proclamation to the German troops and people urging the troops to surrender and the people to begin planting crops. He described the hopelessness of continuing the war and told them that further resistance would only add to the future miseries. In spite of the warning, the Germans, through the medium of the Gestapo and S. S. troops, continued to fight.

The 332nd strafed enemy motor transportation in the vicinity of Verona, Italy, on April 4, 1945. While strafing, Captain Hugh White was shot down. He was captured by the Germans who at the time were retreating northward out of Italy because of the great Allied offensive. White noted that the Germans were so low on gasoline that they used horses and wagons instead of motor vehicles. Traffic moved at a snail's pace. The British Sixth South African Division caught up with the Germans at Padova, Italy, and released White. He returned to the Group and was sent back to the States three days later.

On April 12 the 332nd Fighter Group lost Lieut. Samuel Leftenant. His ship collided in mid air with a ship flown by

Lieut. James Hall of Washington, D. C., while flying over Russian occupied territory. Both pilots bailed out of their planes but Leftenant was never seen or heard of again.

Lieut. Hall landed safely, was picked up by the Russians, and sent to Russia. There he requested a plane to fly back to the base, but his request was refused. The Russians, for reasons unknown, had specific routes for evacuating Americans from their territories. Although transports left Russia daily for American ports, Hall was sent out of Russia by way of Bucharest.

The first great German capitulation came in Italy. Throughout the winter months the lines in northern Italy had remained static. Neither side had launched any major offensive. In January and February, 1945, there were rumors that the Germans were withdrawing. These rumors, however, could not be substantiated by Allied Intelligence.

In April General Clark announced an Allied spring offensive. At this time the Allied line ran south of Bologna. In mid April the Allied Army launched an attack which resulted in the capture of Bologna on April 21, 1945. The Fifth and Eighth Armies pursued the Germans who fled across the Po valley.

The 332nd Fighter Group also played its part in the final battles of the Italian campaign. On April 23 the 332nd flew two missions. The first mission was escort and target cover for B-24s of the Red force of the 55th and 304th Bomb Wings attacking Padua and Cavarzere, Italy. Upon the completion of the target cover assignment sixteen aircraft of the Group conducted an armed reconnaissance to the Verona, Morostica, Padua, Cavarzere, Staghella, and Legnana areas of northern Italy. The second mission furnished general escort, penetration, and target cover for the Blue force of B-24s of the 55th and 304th Bomb Wings attacking targets in the Padua and Cavarzere areas in Italy.

Meanwhile the Allied Army in the west had contacted the Red Army on the Elbe. The Russians, who had launched a powerful drive on a two hundred mile front from their Oder river position, had made speedy progress. General Dwight D. Eisenhower, describing the war, wrote: "Almost coincidently with our arrival on the Elbe the Red Army launched a powerful westward drive from its positions on the Oder. The attack was on a front of more than two hundred miles. The Red drive made speedy progress everywhere. Its northern flank pushed in the direction of the Danish peninsula, the center towards Berlin, and the southern flank towards the Dresden area. On April 25th patrols of the 69th Division of the V Corps met elements of the Russian Army's 58th Guards Division on the Elbe. This meeting took place at Torgau some seventy-five miles south of Berlin."[1]

While Allied troops were swarming over Germany and swiftly pursuing the retreating Germans in Italy, there were few remaining targets against which the Air Force could be directed without danger of dropping their bombs on Allied troops. As a result, on April 26 the 15th Air Force flew its last mission. This was a Photo Reconnaissance mission to Prague. During the mission three members of the 332nd Fighter Group were credited with destroying four enemy aircraft and one probable. The pilots receiving credit for victories were: Lieut. Jimmie Lanham of Philadelphia, Pennsylvania, who was credited with one enemy plane and one probable; Lieut. Thomas W. Jefferson of Chicago, Illinois, who received two victories and Lieut. Richard A. Simons of White Plains, New York, one victory.

On April 29 the German forces in Italy surrendered to the Allies. This made it impossible for the German First and Nineteenth Armies, just to the north of Italy, to continue fighting and as a result they surrendered to the Allies on May 6, 1945. Meanwhile, on May 1, the 332nd Fighter Group moved further north in Italy to Cattolica, where it prepared for a final offensive. However, plans for the unconditional surrender of Germany were already in the making. On May 7 Admiral

---

[1]From: Crusade in Europe, by Dwight D. Eisenhower. Copyright 1948 by Doubleday & Company, Inc.

Doenitz, the new commander in chief of German Forces, instructed two of his emissaries, Admiral Friedeburg and General Jodl, who had proceeded to General Eisenhower's advanced headquarters at Reims, to sign the unconditional surrender terms. This accomplished, hostilities ceased at midnight May 8, 1945. Thus was brought to an end the greatest war the world has ever known.

With the war in Europe over, the members of the 332nd Fighter Group looked forward to taking the battle to the Japs. Colonel Davis addressed his men soon after Germany surrendered. He remarked: "Our growing pains are over now. We know our job and how to do it. In the Pacific we should be more successful as a result of our experiences in this campaign. I am personally quite happy that this end of the war is over, but we won't be able to really celebrate until we know that the entire war, including the Pacific, has been finished."

CHAPTER XIX

THE 332nd RETURN TO THE STATES

On June 8, 1945, Colonel Benjamin O. Davis, Jr. was awarded the Silver Star for gallantry in combat. This award was presented to him at a farewell ceremony held prior to his departure to the United States for a new assignment as commanding officer of the 477th Composite Group. In his departing speech the Colonel remarked: "Our mission here has been completed. We have fought the war and I think the Group has done very well."

Colonel Davis also received praise for his efficient leadership. General Dean C. Strother, Commanding General of the 15th Air Force Fighter Command, remarked to an Afro War Correspondent. "He is a fine soldier and has done wonders with the 332nd. I am positive that no other man in our Air Corps could have handled this job in the manner he has."

Lieut. Colonel George S. Roberts, Deputy Commander of the Group, succeeded Colonel Davis. Earlier in the war he commanded the 99th Fighter Squadron when Colonel Davis returned to the States to lead the 332nd into combat. At the same time, other changes were made in the staff organization of the Group due to the return of officers to the States. Captain Wendell Lucas of Fairmount Heights, Maryland, succeeded Major William A. Campbell as Commanding Officer of the 99th Fighter Squadron. Captain Bertram Wilson of Brooklyn, New York, was appointed Operations Officer, and Captain Bernard Proctor of Philadelphia, Pennsylvania, succeeded Major Nelson Brooks as Executive Officer of the Group.

While the 332nd waited to be sent back to the States, its members continued to fly practice missions. During these missions the Group lost Lieuts. Charles Squires and James Coleman. Lieut. Squires was killed when he and several other pilots of the 332nd flew up to Pisa shortly after V-E Day to buzz the 92nd Infantry Division. On arrival over the 92nd area, Squires attempted a victory roll while on deck. Just after he started his roll, his plane skidded off course and crashed. Lieut. Coleman, a member of the 100th Squadron, was killed when his plane exploded in mid air while practising divebombing.

In the meantime, on June 21, 1945, Colonel Benjamin O. Davis, Jr. assumed command of the newly activated 477th Composite Group. This group, when completed, was to consist of two bomber squadrons and one pursuit squadron from the 332nd Fighter Group. The remaining squadrons of the 332nd were to be held in strategic reserve. Lieut. General Ira C. Eaker, Acting Commanding General of the Army Air Forces, flew from Washington, D. C., to install Colonel Davis in his new post. Other high officials present at the ceremony were Brigadier General Benjamin O. Davis of the office of Inspector General, European Theatre of Operations, Brigadier General Edgar E. Glenn, and Mr. Truman K. Gibson, Jr., Civilian Aide to the Secretary of War.

General Eaker, who had served as Commander of the Allied Air Force in the Mediterranean Theatre of operation during the war, remarked: "It was upon my personal recommendation and insistence that Colonel Davis is to take command of this group because of the excellent work I saw him do overseas." He stated also that General MacArthur, when asked whether he would accept the 477th Composite Group in the Pacific, replied, "I'll take anybody willing to fight the Japs."

General Benjamin O. Davis, addressing the members of the 477th, said: "The department is sparing no pains to give you the advantage of experience. Your new commanding officer, Colonel Davis, and the officers accompanying him from his former assignment are men fresh from the European Combat zone. Nearly all of them have not only been in combat, but they have been awarded decorations for meritorious services performed in combat.

[146]

Fig. 19.   PILOT   OF   THE   477TH   BOMBER   GROUP
WARMS   UP   PLANE   AT   GODMAN   FIELD,
KENTUCKY

Fig. 20.   B-25   IN   FLIGHT

Fig. 21. LEADERS OF THE 332ND "RED TAILS"

Fig. 22. THE 332ND RETURNS TO THE STATES

"The Jap is a tough soldier, and in most cases he has to be killed. To the veterans of World War I, who may be with you now and have not had combat experience in the present war, I would like to say that the experience of the soldier of the present war is far different from that of yours . . . The only people who know how to fight this war to the best advantage are the people who have had actual combat experience with the enemy. I wish to congratulate you on the calibre of the officers to be assigned to you. They have the confidence of the Department; they have the respect of the men they have fought with and against. I urge you to give them your wholehearted loyalty, support, and maximum effort to bring about a victory."

The great surprise came on July 1, 1945, when Colonel Davis was appointed as commanding officer of Godman Field. This gave him the distinction of being the first Negro to command an Army Air Force base in the United States. He assumed his new command with the same enthusiasm and confidence that he portrayed in his command of the 99th Fighter Squadron and the 332nd Fighter Group. Immediately he set about to build up Godman Field by soliciting experienced ground officers and enlisted men from Tuskegee Army Air Field. To strengthen the 477th Composite Group he also had a large number of veteran pilots stationed at Tuskegee transferred to Godman.

Shortly after this Colonel Davis addressed a large gathering at Tuskegee Army Air Field. The occasion was the fourth anniversary of the field. "I am very proud," he said, "to have been at one time a part of this training center and am deeply grateful for all that I learned here. It would be relatively easy to heap praise upon praise for your accomplishments. I could state that a very definite and concrete contribution to the war effort has been made here at Tuskegee. Fortunately, this is completely unnecessary. The men whom you have trained here have produced an indelible record reflecting the accomplishments of Tuskegee. It is a record written in the blood of our own and that of our enemies, in Sicily, Italy, France, Greece, Yugoslavia,

Albania, Bulgaria, Hungary, Austria, Czechoslovakia, Poland, and Germany. It is a record that stands on its own, and empty words would not add to it.

"All America hates war. It is basic American philosophy not to seek war, but to prevent it. This has been true from the shot heard around the world at Lexington to the treachery of Pearl Harbor. It is also true, and I am proud to say, that whenever there has been war, American Negroes have been more than willing to carry their share. Bunker Hill, San Juan, the Argonne Forest, Bataan, and the shores of Normandy are all drenched with the blood of Negroes who made the supreme sacrifice for the right to be called Americans without qualification."

In July, 1945, the 99th Fighter Squadron returned to the States and was reassigned to the 477th Composite Group. Major William A. Campbell, who had commanded the squadron overseas, was reassigned to command the squadron. The remaining squadrons of the 332nd Fighter Group led by Lieut. Colonel Roberts arrived at Pier 15, Staten Island, New York, aboard the S. S. Levi Woodbury on October 17, 1945. Here the members of the Group were heartily received by a crowd who had gathered to welcome them. As soon as disembarkation was completed, the 332nd was sent to Camp Kilmer, New Jersey, where is was deactivated. A large percentage of its enlisted personnel was discharged while the remainder were given extended leave before being reassigned to new stations. Most of the officers were reassigned either to Tuskegee Army Air Field or Godman Field.

Colonel Davis was also able to reassign a large percentage of the experienced staff personnel of the 332nd to responsible positions at Godman Field. Major Edward Gleed, who had served as Operation Officer with the 332nd, was assigned as Operation Officer for the 477th Composite Group. Major Elmer Jones, who commanded the 523rd Air Service Group in Italy, was assigned to lead the 387th Air Service Group. Major Andrew Turner, who commanded the 100th Fighter Squadron in combat, was appointed Deputy Group Commander. Major Vance N. Marchbanks, Group Surgeon of the 332nd Fighter Group, was appointed to that position in the 477th Composite Group. Major Thomas J. Money assumed the position of Executive Officer of the new group. Captain John R. Beverly was appointed Group Intelligence Officer, and Captain Omar Blair was assigned to command the Material Squadron of the service group.

The 477th Composite Group was transferred from Godman Field to Lockbourne Army Air Base in Columbus, Ohio, on March 13, 1946. On May 1, 1946, it was deactivated and the 332nd Fighter Group was reactivated. A few months later, on August 15, 1946, the 332nd Fighter Group was reorganized into the 332nd Fighter Wing. This organization continued until June 1, 1949, when the 332nd Fighter Wing was deactivated and its personnel was integrated into white organizations throughout the world. The integration of the personnel of Lockbourne Air Base into white organizations was the fulfillment of Colonel Davis's dream of making the experiment "an unqualified success."

CHAPTER XX

STORIES OF PRISONERS OF WAR

To fall in the hands of the enemy and to become a prisoner of war is a hectic experience. Not that all prisoners were treated inhumanely, for they were not. But, no matter how humanely a prisoner was treated, he lived in anticipation of the worst that could happen to him.

One day at Tuskegee I talked with a few men who had experienced the German prison camp. To see these men, jolly and seemingly in excellent health, one would never suspect they had braved the deprivations of German prison camps. However, as I listened to them relate their varied experiences I realized that the Germans treated prisoners of war as prisoners and not as gods or "little bad boys" as we Americans treated captured German soldiers.

Lieut. Alexander Jefferson, one of the smallest pilots of the 332nd Fighter Group and perhaps of the entire United States Army Air Force, was one of these men who experienced the war as a prisoner. It was August 12, 1944, three days before D-day in Southern France when he and several other members of the 332nd fell victim to Nazi guns. On that day the 332nd was assigned to destroy radar stations on the coast of France in preparation for the invasion of ground troops. Upon arrival over the target area the group encountered heavy and accurate flak and machine gun fire. But in spite of the heavy and concentrated enemy fire the group went in to dive bomb and strafe its targets. At this point Lieut. Jefferson began his story. "I started my dive at 15,000 feet and headed straight in for the station. But when I got about two hundred yards from the target a 20 mm shot burst through the floor of my cockpit. Immediately, my plane burst into flames. I kept my control, however, rolled my plane to the left, pushed forward on the stick, and fell out of my plane at about 600 feet. I landed about 200 feet from the target and was immediately picked up by the Germans and taken to the headquarters of a flak battalion.

"Just before my ship was hit Captain Robert H. Daniels' ship was hit by a 20 mm shell. The burst ripped his plane practically apart and sent it spiraling into the water below. But somehow Daniels managed to get out of his plane before it sank. He was later fished out of the water by the Germans and the next day brought into headquarters. Frankly, it made me feel much better to have some one I knew with me. You know, misery loves company.

"On the morning of August 14, about four o'clock, we were taken by two guards to Toulon and later to Marseilles, France. There we were put on a train, which was packed with German civilians and soldiers.

"When we arrived at Orange, France, the tracks were bombed out so we hitch hiked to Lyon. I noticed as we were going along that the Germans were moving all types of equipment and vehicles out of the Rhone valley. Incidentally, the train was strafed once by a P-38 while we were on the way to Orange. The strafing was ineffective, but it forced everybody to jump off the train into the ditches. I also saw B-25s bomb Valence and about forty-five minutes before reaching Lyon B-24s bombed the industrial plants of the city.

"The ride from Lyon up to Frankfort was uneventful except for curious glances from the people. Probably many of them had never seen Negroes before, so naturally they were curious to get a good look at us.

"We passed through Belfort, Mulhouse, Freiburg, Karlsruhe, and Mannheim before reaching Frankfort. At Frankfort we were placed in solitary confinement and later interrogated. The most startling thing about the interrogation is that the interrogators seemed to know more about my outfit than I did. I was shown a booklet, compiled on the 332nd Fighter Group. It contained the names and addresses of nearly all the graduates of Tuskegee, pictures of classes, and approximate dates the pilots arrived overseas. The only thing they didn't seem to know was the number of missions I had.

"We stayed at Frankfort for three days and were then shipped to Wetzlar, about seventy-five miles from Frankfort. Here we got the benefit of the American Red Cross for the first time. We were allowed to take shower baths, given clean bedding and clothing, and given our first hot meal, which consisted of oatmeal, German bread, cocoa, and powdered eggs.

"We stayed in Wetzlar only two days, then with about 300 other prisoners were crowded on a train and for four days and four nights traveled. We were taken off the train at Sagan and held at Stalag Luft III for six months.

"At Stalag Luft III ten officers lived in a room about 16 x 16 feet. We did our own cooking and made our own implements for cooking and eating. Most of the pots and pans were made from cans received in Red Cross parcels. But in spite of the hardship of prison life the morale of the prisoners was rather high. Most of my room mates were southerners. Two were from Georgia, three from Alabama, two from Florida, one from Missouri, and one from Michigan. Although I was a Negro they treated me as one of them. Each man performed a duty, and each day we combined our rations, cooked it together, and shared equally.

"Stalag Luft III was divided into five sections with approximately two thousand men in each section. Altogether there were about 10,000 prisoners. Every morning at 6:30 we were called out to answer roll call.

"The Red Cross parcels, received usually once a week, came in very handy. They not only supplemented the German rations, but often were the only food we received. In the latter part of September each prisoner's ration was cut to half a parcel because the German transportation system was under constant bombardment. This cut in ration hurt us tremendously but we managed to make out.

"For amusement and to help pass away time we played

various games, presented camp shows, and read books from the large library which had been built up by previous prisoners. Two plays that were presented while I was at Stalag Luft were *The Philadelphia Story* and *Kiss and Tell.* They were interesting.

"Saturday night, January 29, 1945, we received orders that we were going to move. This hasty movement was probably due to the fact that the Russian troops had advanced from Warsaw within thirty miles of the camp. We could hear the roar of the big guns.

"The forced march from Stalag Luft III at Sagan was no fun. We marched a distance of about eighty-five kilometers in bitter cold weather. We were guarded by Volksturm guards made up of old men. There was about two and a half feet of snow on the ground and the temperature was about ten degrees below zero. I saw four guards fall out from exhaustion. No one seemed to pay much attention to them and they probably froze to death. Fortunately for us, when we got ready to move the Red Cross gave us new shoes, heavy socks, gloves, scarfs, and new overcoats.

"When we reached Spremberg we were placed in box cars, sixty men to a car. For three days and nights we traveled southward through Dresden, Chemnitz, Plauen, Nürnberg, and finally ended up in Moosburg. Here we were held at Stalag 7-A. The conditions at Stalag 7-A were deplorable. We lived in tents about forty feet wide and one hundred feet long. We slept on the ground as comfortably as possible, but had one faucet for approximately four hundred men. The only satisfaction we had was the Red Cross kept us from starving by sending us parcels regularly.

"Our last few months at Moosburg were spent in almost agony. The intense sweating out what the Germans were eventually going to do with us was torture. We knew the Americans were coming, and feared the Germans might shoot us rather than let us be rescued by the Allies. We also feared that we would be caught in the midst of a battle between the

Americans and the Nazi guards. We watched B-17s bomb Munich one day. It was really a wonderful sight, but after that we feared that we would be victims of such a raid.

"Incidentally, Richard Macon was also shot down the day I was shot down. I met him two days later, but when we arrived at Sagan we were separated. When I arrived at Moosburg I learned that Lieut. Woodrow Morgan, Lieut. Hatchcock, and Lieut. Wilbur Long were there, but we were in different sections and couldn't see each other.

"We stayed at Moosburg until the Third Army arrived and liberated us on April 29, 1945. However, we remained in camp for a week or so, then we were taken to Strasbourg in trucks. Here we boarded a C-47 and were flown to Le Havre, France. We stayed at camp 'Lucky Strike' for approximately five days, then boarded ship for our voyage back to the States. Daniels and I arrived in the States on June 2, 1945, happy that we were safely home again."

After listening to Lieut. Jefferson's interesting narrative of his life as a prisoner of war I wandered into the pool room at Tuskegee Air Base where I found Lieut. Wilbur Long watching a game of pool. Long, a small, slender, light-complexioned, quiet sort of fellow, offered to play me a game. As we shot pool I began to ask questions about the mission on which he was shot down and became a prisoner of war. "Well," he said, "I guess you have heard my story many times. I was one of the fortunate pilots who got shot down and was lucky enough to get back home. Anyway, it was an escort mission to Blechhammer about one hundred and fifty miles east of Berlin. I was hit over the target by flak. My canopy was damaged, my coolant system was messed up, and I received several minor injuries.

"Immediately after regaining my composure I checked over my plane. Figuring that I was not too badly damaged, I decided that I would try to make it back to the base. Several members of my flight warned me that my ship was damaged severely and that I should leave my ship.

"Meantime I was unaware that I was flying in the wrong

[154]

direction. Captain Daniels (John) directed me on course, but a little later my engine began to freeze up, so I made preparations to bail out. But when I attempted to release my canopy I found it was damaged. I informed Captain Daniels I could not release my canopy, so I would have to crash land. He instructed me to find a field and land, that he would pick me up. I found a field that looked rather clear from a high altitude. But as I approached the field for a landing I found it had many obstacles. Skimming over tree tops and dodging through spaces between trees I finally hit the ground and began skidding. From this time on I remember nothing about my landing.

"When I regained consciousness I was running with a large gathering of civilians chasing me. I remembered I had a pistol on me. I also remembered that I had been briefed that pilots caught by the enemy with fire arms were severely beaten and often killed. Therefore, I threw my pistol away. I was overtaken and beaten by the angry mob. However, a group of soldiers arrived in time to save me. The soldiers tried to question me, but I couldn't understand them. A kid who could speak English came up and acted as interpreter. The soldiers searched me and found my extra clip of cartridges. They inquired as to what I did with my gun, where I was from, etc. When they finished questioning me they took me to a small town where a doctor bandaged up my nose, which had been split open, probably by my gun sight when I crashed.

"Shortly afterwards a Hungarian Colonel arrived and endeavored to interrogate me. He, unable to speak English, and I, unable to speak Hungarian, could not understand each other. The Colonel then changed to German. I studied German before entering the Army, so I was able to understand him. I learned that I was in Hungary. When the Colonel asked me questions that I didn't wish to answer I pretended that I couldn't understand him.

"I was told by the Colonel that I was going to be sent to a hospital for treatment. To my surprise I was placed in solitary

[155]

confinement. The next day I was taken to another garrison and again placed in solitary confinement.

"Five days later I was carried to Budapest and placed in a hospital for treatment. I stayed in the hospital for two weeks. But at this time the Allies began their campaign against the city. This angered the Nazis and they took me out of the hospital and threw me in solitary confinement. The following day I was interrogated. I was asked a few questions which I refused to answer. I told the interrogator I could give him only my name, rank, and serial number. Seeing that he was making no headway, the interrogator told me that I didn't know any more than he. Walking to a desk he pulled out a book entitled the 332nd Red Tails. This book contained practically the history of the group from its activation at Tuskegee.

"After I had been interrogated I was placed in a garrison with some more prisoners. I was approached by an inmate dressed as a prisoner. He was particularly interested in Russia. I told him that I never had any contact with the Russians and knew very little about them.

"Finally the inmate revealed that he had lived many years in America. He stated he knew how Negroes were treated in the United States, but couldn't understand why Negroes were so faithful to such a country.

"I asked him why they were so hard on the Jews, who wanted life, liberty, and happiness like other people. He responded that the Jews had sold Germany out after the last war, and that they had hoarded all the capital of Germany. I inquired as to why they attacked Poland and occupied all the smaller countries of Europe. He maintained that the Germans were the underdogs of Europe, that they were allowed to travel through only one street of Poland to get to Danzig, and the Poles, backed up by France and Britain, made fun of them. He also alleged that the Germans were not treated fairly in sharing the markets of the world like other countries.

"He was interested in knowing what the United States was planning to do with Germany should she win the war. He had heard that the United States planned to divide Germany into two or three smaller countries. I told him that I was only an ordinary soldier and knew nothing of the plans of the United States.

"The next day I was put on a box car with a group of prisoners and sent to Stalag Luft III. Here I met Floyd Thompson and Lewis C. Smith. I also learned that several other members of the 332nd were also imprisoned here, but since this camp was divided into several compounds, each surrounded by high barbed wire fences, we never met while there.

"On July 29 we were marched out of Stalag Luft III. After a forced march of seventy-five or eighty kilometers we were placed on a train and shipped to Moosburg. We remained here until April 29th when we were liberated by the Third Army."

One morning I ventured over to Lieut. Harold Brown's room to chat with him. I found Brown still in bed though it was nearly eleven o'clock. Brown, a rather nice looking youngster, appeared too young to be a veteran combat pilot. Although always pleasant and friendly, his mannerism gave him the appearance of a spoiled only child. Brown and I talked for a while about various things, but finally we got around to the usual subject of combat. "You know," he said, "we had a lot of good pilots in the 99th, but in my opinion our squadron commander, Major Campbell, was the best pilot of the Squadron and Group. He loved to fly and was a damn good pilot. He had so much nerve! He led so many missions Colonel Davis grounded him. I'll never forget the mission he led when I went down.

"On March 14, 1945, we went on a strafing mission to strafe enemy railroads between Brux and Stety. I flew Major Campbell wing that day. Anyway, we were strafing a railroad when we spotted a locomotive. One by one we peeled off from formation and dived down on the locomotive that was steaming down the tracks trying to outrun us. I went in with my guns opened up, but I had my mind so set on hitting my target I allowed my plane to come too close to the locomotive.

As I pulled up the locomotive exploded. My ship was severely damaged. I managed to climb up to approximately 20,000 feet and headed for Yugoslavia, friendly territory. En route my ship began to act up. I tried to keep it under control, but after falling to about 14,000 feet I decided to jump.

"I landed on a snow covered mountain slope between a group of tall pine trees. I received a few minor lacerations, otherwise I wasn't hurt. Immediately upon hitting the ground I decided to get out of the area as quickly as possible, because I knew someone must have seen me bail out and would investigate.

"I started out with the idea of reaching Yugoslavia. After walking for approximately twenty minutes I was picked up by some civilian policemen and turned over to some German soldiers.

"The next morning I was put on a train and carried to a small town about forty-five kilometers from where I was captured. That evening, I was taken out of jail, put on a bus and carried to a private Air Field. I remained here eight days. During my stay here a bomber crew joined me. Four days later we were placed on a train and sent to Regensburg and from there to Nürnberg.

"We were interrogated at Nürnberg and again put on a train headed for Frankfort on the Main. However, due to the destruction of the rail system by the Allies we were forced to return to Nürnberg. On my return to Nürnberg I met Lieut. Lincoln Hudson who had been shot down on March 23. The same evening I was carried across town and placed in a German prison camp called Stalag Luft III. A few days later Hudson joined me. While at Stalag Luft III, I met Lieut. Iles and Lieut. Gorham.

"Early in April the Germans decided to move the personnel of the camp because Allied Forces were closing in fast. We were marched about 150 kilometers to Moosburg where we were imprisoned at Stalag Luft VII-A. I met several officers of the 332nd here. They were Lieuts. Lloyd S. Hathcock of Peoria,

Illinois, who was shot down over Rome in June, 1944, Robert H. Daniels, Jr., who was shot down over Toulon in August, 1944, Kenneth I. Williams, who was shot down over Athens, Wilbur F. Long, shot down over Blechhammer in September, 1944, Carrol S. Woods, shot down over Athens, Greece, on October 6, 1944, Captain Armour McDaniel, shot down over Berlin on March 24, 1945, Walter McCreary, shot down over Hungary, Roger B. Gaither, shot down over Budapest, Hungary, Richard Macon, shot down over Montpellier, France, Thurston L. Gaines, Jr., shot down over Nürnberg, Clarence N. Driver, shot down over Linz on March 25, 1945, Woodrow F. Morgan, shot down over Rome, Alexander Jefferson, shot down over Toulon, France, and Newman Golden, shot down over the Alps near Linz, Austria, on March 20, 1945.

"My interrogation at Nürnberg revealed how thoroughly the German Intelligence Department gathered information. The interrogators knew practically everything about the 332nd except the range of the P-51 we flew. After telling me the history of my squadron the interrogator remarked: 'Brown, I heard that Captain Toppins has returned from his leave and has resumed flying. He was lucky in shooting down several of our planes. This time we intend to sack him up.'

" 'Tell me, Brown, why are you fellows so willing to fight for the United States? I know how colored people are treated in the United States and especially in the South. We are considered enemies of the United States, and you fellows are dying for the United States, yet our boys receive better treatment in the United States than you. I can't understand you fellows!' "

One of my acquaintances at Tuskegee was Lieut. Newman C. Golden, a Cincinnati, Ohio, youth. He was inducted into the army at Patterson Field, Ohio, on October 14, 1942. He applied for cadet training and was sent to Tuskegee where he was graduated as a Flight Officer and sent overseas as a replacement for the 99th Fighter Squadron on January 25, 1945. While flying his thirteenth mission on March 20, 1945, his plane developed engine trouble. In the words of Golden: "I bailed out about fifty miles west of Linz, Austria. When I pulled my chute I became entangled in the cord and received a very bad injury to my left knee. I was unable to walk. After lying on the ground for about ten minutes I saw a small child playing nearby, so I yelled at him. He ran home and a little later returned with his parents, who disarmed me and carried me to their farm house. Here I was held until some soldiers arrived and carried me off to jail. After two days I was sent to Nürnberg, Germany. I stayed at Nürnberg a week then was moved to Stalag Luft VII-A at Moosburg. I remained at Moosburg until April 29, 1945, when I was liberated by General Patton's Third Army, 14th Armored Division."

CHAPTER XXI

"THE HARD WAY"

When it was decided that a segregated base would be established for Negroes, high Army officials tried to explain their actions. They contended that the humiliation and possible maltreatment Negro cadets would face at unsegregated Army Air Force schools would hinder them in developing the self confidence and initiative necessary as pilots.

When the construction of Tuskegee Army Air Base began it was foreseen that a number of experienced white officers and enlisted men would be needed at the base until Negroes were sufficiently trained to operate the base. With this in mind, plans were drawn that provided for separate quarters and separate mess for white and Negro personnel. It was then realized by those who had argued against the establishment of a segregated base for Negroes that the Army, rather than shelter Negro soldiers from the humiliation and practices that tended to make them feel inferior, had deliberately planned such a program. Judge William H. Hastie wrote in regard to the contemplated set-up at Tuskegee: "I protested against the segregation within the segregated training center. I pointed out that if the white officers and enlisted men wanted such segregation they were obviously unfit to train Negroes. Moreover, the psychological effect upon Negro officers and enlisted men was bound to be catastrophic. My representations were unavailing and the plan of racial segregation within the post was carried out."[1]

Negroes were also told in the establishment of Tuskegee Army Air Base that Negro officers and enlisted men would replace the white personnel as rapidly as possible. Yet, throughout the entire existence of the base, no substantial substitutions were made, though there were numerous Negroes qualified for each position at the field. Negro officers for the most part were relegated to positions that gave them little chance for promotion. While Negro officers were denied equal opportunities for service and advancement they witnessed rapid advancement of young white officers, who were often less qualified.

Although Colonel Parrish was more tactful in handling the racial and social problems at Tuskegee than Colonel Kimble, he made no substantial changes in the operation of the base. There still remained numerous practices that tended to cause resentment by the Negro personnel.

In the spring of 1944 Colonel Parrish called an assembly to introduce the officer personnel of the field. There were assistants galore, assistant to the assistant Mess officer, assistant to the assistant Supply officer, assistant to this, to that, and even assistants to a makeshift position as Post Beautification officer— so many, in fact, that it was actually humiliating. Those who had gone through the rigors of training at the various officers' training schools felt useless and despondent. Even though hundreds of able bodied men were sitting around at Tuskegee doing practically nothing, the army was in dire need of men on the battlefield.

The tension over the discriminatory practice at Tuskegee received publicity when an article published by the *Pittsburgh Courier* on September 16, 1944, related the "Inside Story of Tuskegee." The article written by an anonymous "Jack Day" was highly colored with mockery, but basically it expressed vividly the practices at Tuskegee. The odious practices reached such proportions that Lieut. James S. Mosley of Philadelphia, Pennsylvania, felt it necessary to submit a letter of resignation while still in pilot training. The resignation read as follows:

"Not believing in war primarily, I relinquished any rights I might have had, as a citizen, to adhere to this ideal by submitting to the draft. In doing so, I compromised certain ideals which I considered fundamental in human relations. In return for this compromise, along with thousands of others, I sincerely anticipated correspondingly progressive advances in policy and

Fig. 23.   LIEUTENANT HARVEY AND MEMBERS OF
THE 332ND GUNNERY TEAM

Fig. 24.   MAJOR WILLIAM A. CAMPBELL AND AIR-
MAN BEFORE TAKEOFF

Fig. 26. MAJOR ANDREW D. TURNER

Fig. 25. CAPTAIN EDWARD TOPPINS

practice, relative to the treatment of minority segments of the army. The Negro soldier specifically.

"The war aims were directed primarily at uprooting the evils of man against man. These evils were described under varied titles, Nazism, Fascism, etc. Notwithstanding, I find many of the basic evils of the two aforementioned conditions existing within the structure of our army. Worse, there is no definite move under way for the abolition of these practices. Namely, the establishment of segregation and the accompanying evils of discrimination, which literally divides the army into a caste system. Proof that it is discriminatory as well as segregated is found in the fact that it is army policy never to have members of the non-white army command units of the white. Though the antithesis is so frequent as to become odd indeed to find even a non-white in command of a non-white unit.

"These discriminatory practices together with the failure of the army to amply provide protection for personnel in hostile communities . . . has led me to ponder seriously the cause for which so many sacrifice so much."

Many members of the 99th Fighter Squadron and the 332nd Fighter Group found Tuskegee a very disheartening place when they returned from combat. Though they had risked their lives fighting for their country, they were given no assignments to keep them occupied. Even Colonel Roberts, who had commanded the 99th Fighter Squadron and the 332nd Fighter Group in combat, met with the same degrading treatment. Even though he was quite capable as a leader, administrator, and combat pilot, he was assigned as Bachelor Quarters Officer, a position that the lowest non-commissioned officer could have held. Of course, such an assignment would have been considered an insult to a white officer of equal experience and rank.

The opposition to the segregated base at Tuskegee reached its climax in late 1945, when President Patterson of Tuskegee Institute requested the War Department to consider other locations for a peacetime base for Negro Airmen. In a telegram to the Chief of Staff at the War Department he advised:

[163]

"Acting on advice which I regarded as reliable and personally believing that participation of Negroes in the Army Air Force could be encouraged and effectively aided by the use of the splendid facilities and relationship developed during the war at Tuskegee Army Air Field, I suggested to you that tactical reserve units for peace time be based at this government owned and operated field.

"Information now received indicates objections by an important percentage of Negro flying officers to basing of such tactical units at the field.

"I therefore withdraw my suggestion that this be done. I do not believe that the best interest of the Negro in the Army Air Force will be served if the Group were stationed in the community with the personnel of the said group displeased with the location."

The segregated program of the Air Force also affected Negro pilots in combat. The job of commanding the 99th Fighter Squadron and the 332nd Fighter Group was made difficult by the segregated policy of the War Department. While in combat, Colonel Davis often found himself short of replacements. A large number of his men were required to fly more than one hundred missions while white pilots were being sent back to the United States upon completing fifty missions. At the same time, while he was in dire need of replacements, many white organizations had more pilots than they could use. Even then he could not draw from these organizations to fill his shortage. This factor more than anything else kept the morale of his pilots low.

Recognition of the ability of Negro pilots also came slowly. Soon after the 99th entered combat its pilots were unjustly criticized for not shooting down enemy aircraft they did not contact. Colonel Davis, relating the experiences of the 332nd in combat, said: "At first we were not called upon to fly on important missions because high Air Force commanders had little confidence in us. When white crewmen returned from mission after mission and praised us for our 'Close Support' and requested that we fly as escort on other missions, we began to gain recognition as a competent outfit. Soon we began to get more missions and later we were treated as any other outfit."

The men proved to be competent pilots in spite of the hardship encountered both in the States and in combat. Colonel Noel F. Parrish, in discussing the success of the flying school, said: "How good were our pilots? We heard the question so much we could hear it in our sleep. How good is any pilot? Our men were good enough to graduate from any flying school in the country . . . we made sure of that . . . and working together we proved it. We emphasized that a pilot or a man of whatever color, size, or shape is just as good as he proves himself to be. Men, and particularly pilots, have to be considered as individuals. We have had some of the worse pilots in the world right here and we have had and still have some of the best. In the first place, they flew and fought as men. They may have been classified as Negroes. They may have been at times abused as Negroes. They may have had pretty good alibis for being failures if they wanted to use these alibis, or they may have been proud of their group as the only one like it in the world, as they had a right to be. But when the test came they had to fly and fight just as men, American men against a common enemy."

Lieut. General Ira C. Eaker, Deputy Commander of the Army Air Forces, who personally witnessed Negro pilots in combat, said: "They carried out the missions assigned to them and they have destroyed enemy aircraft both in the air and on the ground. By their efforts and performances, they have won a place on the great Air Force team. They came on the hard way."

CHAPTER XXII

THE INTEGRATED AIR FORCE

When the War Department announced that Lockbourne Army Air Base would be deactivated and its personnel integrated into white organizations, there were many who were not too optimistic as to the actual plans of the Department for Negroes. Many who remembered the wholesale discharge of Negroes after World War I, and the treatment of Negroes in the Armed Services prior to World War II, felt that it was the beginning of a movement to discharge Negroes from the Army Air Force. It was said that from the beginning of this country Negroes have readily accepted the fact that this is their country and have been among the first to volunteer in times of national crisis. In each of the wars the United States has had to fight, Negroes have been denied the privilege of fighting until the shortage of manpower and initial failures made it necessary. Nevertheless, the heroic records of Negroes in each of the wars still did not enable them to have the privilege of remaining in the army after the wars.

Some felt this policy was still being carried out in regard to Negro personnel of the Air Force. It was pointed out that the only Negro bomber group had already been disbanded, that practically all of the navigators, bombardiers, gunners, and pilots of the group were either discharged or transferred to pursuit flying. Under the proposed integration program the only all Negro combat Air Force group and field were to be deactivated. Thus, it was concluded that the Negro airmen, like their forefathers who fought in all the other wars, were also not wanted in the peacetime army.

There were many who felt that integration would not work because the Air Force was not ready for integration. They contended that the integration of Negroes into white organizations would only result in another form of segregation and discrimination and only a few Negroes would be permitted to remain in the service. Those few, they reasoned, would be relegated to the lowest positions and given little opportunity for advancement and leadership. It was also said that even Colonel Davis, who had proved his ability as a soldier and leader, would meet the same fate.

The integrated program was adopted in spite of the pessimism of those who felt that it would not work. On May 11, 1949, a screening board headed by Colonel Davis began screening, individually, all the personnel of the base. On June 1, 1949, Lockbourne Army Air Base was deactivated and its personnel was assigned to Air Bases throughout the United States, the European Command, the Alaskan Air Command, and the Far East Air Command.

The progress of the integration program advanced beyond the hope of the most optimistic exponents of integration. To a large extent those reassigned were received at their new bases as American soldiers and given assignments according to their abilities. Negro officers and enlisted men were given the same privileges as whites and treated as individuals rather than as a race.

Negro pilots were not only integrated into white organizations, but some were assigned as instructors of air cadets. The work of Captain Vernon V. Haywood, Lieuts. Lewis Lynch and John Whitehead at Williams Army Air Base, Arizona, is an example of the acceptance of Negroes at a once segregated base. These men fought with the 332nd Fighter Group during World War II. When Lockbourne Air Base was deactivated they were given instructions in flying jet planes and later assigned as cadet instructors at Williams Air Base.

The war in Korea is also revealing the success of the integrated program. Many of the former members of the 99th Fighter Squadron and the 332nd Fighter Group are distinguishing themselves. It has been estimated that at least twenty-one

Negro pilots and hundreds of enlisted men are doing their share in the battle of Korea. Lieut. James F. Harvey, Jr., one of the first jet pilots to see action in the war, is a former member of the 99th Fighter Squadron. His squadron commander, Major "Squire" Williams of Texas, commented to a War Correspondent, "Harv is one of the best officers I've ever had, and as a man, I don't think I've ever known one I respect more . . . He's a fine pilot, dependable in every way. As to his being a Negro, the only trouble we've ever had about that was when some stupid G. I. made tactless remarks about his race in his presence. The rest of the pilots wanted to take those men apart, but Harv just shrugged it all off . . . We have two Negro pilots in our Group, and both of them are among the most popular men in the outfit."[1] The other pilot was reported as Lieut. Edward P. Drummond of Philadelphia, Pennsylvania.

Braddford Laws, Far East Correspondent for *The Afro-American,* writing from Korea, commented: "Here in Korea as throughout the entire U. S. Far East Air Force colored personnel have long been assigned according to their skill and abilities . . . The Air Force exhibit the true democracy that colored Americans have longed to see in action. There are colored section chiefs, Non-Coms., chief clerks, radio operators, airplane technicians, etc., working together in a common cause—freedom."[2]

Some of the men who served under Colonel Davis criticized the Colonel because they felt his standards were too rigid in combat. They related that when white pilots did nothing but fly combat missions they were required to keep their areas clean, their clothes cleaned and pressed, and remain tidy at all times. Some jokingly said that Colonel Davis never could forget his West Point training—that he was a soldier twenty-four hours a day—"even while asleep."

The men now serving in the integrated Air Force give credit to Colonel Davis for much of their success. Captain Charles W. Dryden, a veteran combat pilot of the 99th Fighter Squadron, related to a correspondent in Korea that the rigid training they received under Colonel Davis fitted them for integration "by making us toe the mark in every detail." He further stated they were prepared for anything from precise army social courtesies to combat flying. Another veteran pilot related to the same correspondent: "We used to think sometimes that our subordinates and superiors were incompetent. We used to say we just weren't ready yet, but we were living in a little close room and did not know what went on in the rest of the house. Now the men can compare and they all have the highest regard for Colonel Benjamin O. Davis, Jr., who flew according to the rules, but who was most fair."[3]

Lieut. James Harvey, expressing his views on the success of the integration program, said: "It is not necessarily the individuals who make for social prejudice; it is the environment they live in.

"I know that the pilots of my outfit won't change when we get back. They know me, and I think they like me for what I am. But the folks back home, will they let those men continue to be my friends back in the States? It will be pretty hard to do, a tough thing to buck, I'm afraid.

"One thing I am sure of, none of these boys here in this outfit would ever let me down in any way. Perhaps my wife and I can't go out to the restaurants or hotels with them in some parts of America, not because they don't want to, but because of the long-standing prejudices and customs that are hard to go against. Still, I feel sure I could count on everyone personally."[4]

Although the integrated program is proving to be very successful there still remains much to be done. There will continue to be many who will be hesitant to accept the fact that the color of a man's skin, his race or religion, does not determine his ability as a soldier. There will continue to be those who will resent being placed in unsegregated organizations. However, the door is now open for qualified Negro youths who may aspire to become members of the United States Army Air Force. The job of these men will not be an easy one. They must display the same willingness to make the supreme sacrifice for their country as their predecessors of the 99th Fighter Squadron and the 332nd Fighter Group. The integration program will require patience, understanding, and tolerance. The story of the hardship Negro youths encountered before being accepted by the Air Corps and the records of the 99th Squadron and 332nd Group should be an inspiration for future generations.

CHAPTER XXIII

LEADERS OF MEN

Colonel Benjamin O. Davis

No doubt the most outstanding member of the 99th Fighter Squadron and the 332nd Fighter Group was Colonel Benjamin O. Davis, Jr. Colonel Davis was born in Wilberforce, Ohio, where his father was an instructor of Military Science and Tactics at Wilberforce University. After completing high school, Colonel Davis entered Western Reserve in Cleveland, Ohio, but later transferred to the University of Chicago. His impressive record at the University of Chicago led Oscar Depriest, former Republican Congressman of Illinois, to appoint him to West Point Military Academy. In June, 1936, he was graduated from West Point with the distinction of being the first Negro to graduate from that institution in forty-seven years.

After a short assignment at Fort Bennings, Georgia, Colonel Davis was transferred to Tuskegee Institute to teach military science and tactics. This assignment lasted until the spring of 1941 when he was sent to Fort Riley, Kansas, to become military aide to his father, Brigadier General Benjamin O. Davis. This assignment was also brief, for in July, 1941, he was accepted as a cadet by the Army Air Force and sent to Tuskegee for pilot training.

Upon receiving his wings as an Air Force pilot in March, 1942, Colonel Davis was assigned to the newly activated 99th Fighter Squadron. On August 27, 1942, he was elevated to the command of the 99th and in April, 1943, carried the squadron overseas. His assignment with the 99th was terminated in September, 1943, when he was recalled to the States to assume command of the 332nd Fighter Group. He led the

[171]

332nd overseas in January, 1944, and commanded it until hostilities in Europe ceased.

In June, 1945, Colonel Davis returned to the United States and on July 21 was appointed to command the newly activated 477th Composite Group which consisted of two bomber squadrons and one fighter squadron. A week later, on July 1, he became the first Negro to command a military post in the United States, when he assumed command of Godman Field. On March 13, 1946, the entire personnel of Godman Field was transferred to Lockbourne Army Air Base in Columbus, Ohio, and Colonel Davis was appointed to command the base. Here the 477th Composite Group was reorganized into the 332nd Fighter Group on May 1, 1946. A few months later, on August 15, the 332nd Fighter Group was reorganized into the 332nd Fighter Wing and operated as such until July, 1949, when Lockbourne Air Base was deactivated and its personnel integrated into white organizations throughout the world.

George S. Roberts

Next to Colonel Davis and one of the men mostly responsible for the success of Negro airmen in combat was Lieut. Colonel George Spencer Roberts. "Spanky," as he was known by his comrades, was born and reared in Fairmount, West Virginia. He attended West Virginia State where he earned a private pilot's license under the civilian aviation program. Roberts was a member of the first class to be commissioned at Tuskegee and, shortly after receiving his wings, was appointed as Commanding Officer of the 99th Fighter Squadron. In August, 1942, Colonel Davis took over the command of the 99th and Roberts became the squadron's operation officer. When Colonel Davis returned to the States in September, 1943, to command the 332nd Group, Roberts again assumed command of the 99th. On June 9, 1945, Roberts was elevated to the command of the 332nd Fighter Group. This job was administrative in nature because the war in Europe was over and little flying was being done. He brought the 332nd Fighter Group back to

[172]

the States in October, 1945, and saw it deactivated at Camp Kilmer, New Jersey.

Charles B. Hall

Perhaps Captain Charles B. Hall of Brazil, Indiana, received more fame as a pilot than any Negro other than Colonel Davis. Before entering the Army, Hall was a student at Illinois State Teachers College. Like thousands of young men he gave up his studies to enlist in the Army. He was accepted for aviation cadet training in 1941 and was commissioned with the fourth class graduated from Tuskegee Army Air Field.

On July 2, 1943, Hall destroyed a Focke-Wulf 190 over Castelvetrano. This gave him the honor of being the first Negro to destroy an enemy aircraft in aerial combat. For this accomplishment he was personally congratulated by General Dwight D. Eisenhower, Allied Commander in Chief, Major General Doolittle, Commanding Officer of the 8th Air Force, General Carl Spaatz, Commander of the United States Strategic Air Force, and Air Marshal Cunningham of the Royal Air Force. On landing at the field, General Eisenhower said, "I want to see the pilot who shot down that Jerry." This was a great honor for a youth who only a few years before was studying to be a teacher.

Success and more glory, however, were in store for Hall. On January 28, 1944, while leading a flight of eight planes on patrol in the Anzio area, a flight of enemy aircraft was encountered. Hall destroyed two of the enemy aircraft. For this feat he was awarded the Distinguished Flying Cross. His citation read as follows:

12th Air Force—Charles B. Hall

Captain, Air Corps—79th Fighter Group

"For extraordinary achievement while participating in aerial flight as pilot of a P-40 type aircraft.

"On 28 January 1944, while leading an eight plane patrol over Anzio, Italy, Captain Hall sighted six FW-190 and ME-109 preparing to strafe Allied ground troops. Attacking so aggressively that he completely disorganized

[173]

the enemy formation, Captain Hall shot down two enemy aircraft and his comrades destroyed two FW-190s and dispersed the remainder without loss or damage to the P-40s. On many missions throughout the Sicilian and Italian campaign, his steadfast devotion to duty and outstanding proficiency as a combat pilot has reflected great credit upon himself and the armed forces of the United States."

Although Hall gained fame practically over night, he remained modest and regular. One night while we were lounging around "shooting the breeze" I asked Hall if he intended to write about his experiences in combat. "No," he replied. "Frankly, I don't think I have done anything unusual. True, I shot down a few enemy planes, but compare my score with that of many white pilots, especially those pilots who flew for the 8th Air Force. They frequently encountered enemy aircraft and gained many victories. The only reason I received so much publicity was because I am the first Negro to have shot down an enemy plane in aerial combat. You know, there were many whites who thought Negroes could not master swift moving planes under combat conditions. When I shot down a plane they were surprised, and it changed their minds. Furthermore, I wouldn't feel right if someone writes about me and ignores the hundreds of other fellows who did as much as I to make the 99th Fighter Squadron and the 332nd Fighter Group successful in combat."

William A. Campbell

There were many pilots of the 332nd Fighter Group who praised Major William A. Campbell as the best flight leader of the group. Everyone who flew with him respected him for his aggressiveness and bravery. Campbell, a tall, slender, jovial lad, was one of the local boys at Tuskegee. He was born and reared at Tuskegee Institute only ten miles from the flying field. After completing high school at Tuskegee, he enrolled at Tuskegee Institute, where he received a degree of Bachelor of Science in Business Administration. He enlisted in the Army as an aviation cadet in February, 1942, and won his wings on July 3, 1942. He was assigned to the 99th Fighter Squadron and in April, 1943, was sent overseas with the Squadron.

After completing his tour of duty, Campbell returned to the United States on December 8, 1943. After a short stay at home he became bored with inactivity and requested more combat duty He returned to combat and, shortly after rejoining the 99th, was made its commanding officer. In his new assignment he displayed leadership and bravery that brought him a promotion to Major.

At the completion of his second tour Campbell was credited with 106 combat missions. He was awarded the Distinguished Flying Cross with one oak leaf cluster and the air medal with nine clusters. Even then he was neither tired of fighting nor satisfied to rest on his laurels. When Colonel Davis requested volunteers to aid him in leading the 477th Composite Group into combat against the Japs, Campbell was among the first to volunteer. However, the war in the Pacific ended before the 477th could be sent overseas and Campbell thereby lost the chance of fighting the Japs.

Edward L. Toppins

One cannot speak of the merits of Negro airmen in World War II without mentioning Captain Edward L. Toppins. Toppins was born in Mississippi. At an early age he moved with his parents to San Francisco, California. After completing his elementary training he entered Los Angeles Junior College, from which he was graduated. While still a student at the University of San Francisco Toppins learned that the Army Air Force was accepting Negroes as cadets. He applied for cadet training at Tuskegee Army Air Field.

While in training as a cadet Toppins cracked up a trainer plane that put him in a hospital for several months. Many less stout hearted men would have given up the idea of winning wings, but not Toppins. He was determined to become a pilot and returned to flying. On September 6, 1942, Toppins was commissioned as a Second Lieut. in the Army Air Corps.

Toppins was one of the first four replacement pilots to join the 99th Fighter Squadron in combat. As a member of the 99th Fighter Squadron and the 332nd Fighter Group, he flew 141 missions over Pantelleria, Sicily, Italy, Southern France, Germany, Austria, Yugoslavia, Greece, Bulgaria, Poland, Czechoslovakia, and Romania. He was officially credited with destroying four enemy aircraft in aerial combat and one probable. For this he was awarded the Distinguished Flying Cross, the Air Medal with five clusters, the E. T. O. ribbon with seven battle stars, the American Defense, and the Victory Medal.

If there ever was a pilot who was confident in his ability to shoot down any enemy pilot who dared to do battle with him, it was Toppins. Whenever he flew he was out to shoot down an enemy plane. The Germans learned this after he had shot down several of their planes. Lieut. Harold H. Brown, a member of the 99th Fighter Squadron, who was captured by the Germans upon crash landing in enemy territory, related that a German intelligence officer promised that Nazi pilots would get Toppins if it was the last thing they did. In spite of this promise, Toppins completed his tour and returned to the States.

At Tuskegee Toppins, relating his most memorable mission, said: "One day we were assigned to fly an escort mission to Austria. My flight consisted of Lieut. Leonard Jackson, Lieut. Alva Temple, Lieut. Herber Houston, and myself. On arriving over Lake Balaton we found the sky covered with clouds of varying layers. This was excellent cover for attacking enemy aircraft. We were flying P-51s.

"Shortly afterwards, we observed some enemy aircraft dodging into some clouds above us and at a distance. Immediately we dropped our wing tanks and I led the flight to investigate three ME-109s that had been cavorting high above us since we entered enemy territory.

"The investigation turned into a thirty minute chase, something unusual in aerial combat. Starting at 25,000 feet with everything to the firewall, we slowly closed in on them, both in altitude and distance, despite their 10,000 feet altitude advantage. At 41,000 feet with us just out of range, Jerry decided he could not outclimb us and decided to try and outdive us. The superiority of our ships was so evident that I designated a target for each member of the flight as we jockeyed for position on their tails. Two of the three were confirmed victories and the other a probable. Lieut. Leonard Jackson was credited with one enemy plane and I the others. Having flown the P-40 during most of my tour of duty it was a great thrill to fly a ship which gave me such an overwhelming mastery of the engagement."

Wendell C. Pruitt

There came to Tuskegee in the early part of the war a tall, handsome, Indian featured youngster who was eager to become a pilot. Like all other cadets, he worried from day to day that he would be "washed out." Months passed and he gained more and more confidence in his ability to fly. Then came graduation day and, finally, combat. Soon his uncanny ability to maneuver his plane became so noticeable by other pilots of the group that he became the envy of those who flew with him. This pilot was Captain Wendell O. Pruitt of St. Louis, Missouri.

Pruitt seemingly was cut out for flying. He took chances that the boldest and most experienced pilots dared not take. Even professional acrobatic pilots were cautious in performing stunts that Pruitt did nonchalantly. He scraped roofs of buildings with the wheels of his plane while flying at a very fast rate; slow rolled his plane so close to deck that his wings missed the ground by only a few inches. Pruitt seemed to have little or no premium on his life. He attacked a group of enemy planes with the same lack of caution that he attacked a single enemy ship. Lieut. Lee Archer, who often flew as wingman for Pruitt, and a very good pilot in his own right, often related this story of how he almost met death trying to follow Pruitt.

"One day after registering five victories between us, Pruitt and I went home feeling very good. On approaching the base we decided to do a little acrobatics. It was the custom of the pilots of our group to perform a slow roll over the field when they gained victories. Anyway, we buzzed the field twice. Then

[177]

we decided to make a victory roll. It is almost a habit for all pilots to make a slow roll from the left. Pruitt was left handed and did his rolls from the right. I did not think of this and followed Pruitt in almost on deck. As he rolled his plane to the right I by habit rolled mine to the left. My plane slid under Pruitt's plane while I was upside down. My prop stalled and as I fell out of my roll my plane's wing missed the ground by only a few inches. I was through for that day and today consider myself one of the luckiest pilots in the world."

It was alleged by members of the 332nd Fighter Group that not long after the group arrived overseas Captain Pruitt, together with Lieuts. Lee Archer, Vernon Haywood, and Alfonso W. Davis, Jr., were reported to Colonel Davis for performing acrobatics over Naples, Italy. Colonel Davis did not approve of his pilots performing acrobatics because he was short of pilots and felt that acrobatics were too risky. He therefore, upon receiving the report, ordered Captain Gleed, the 302nd Squadron Commander, to court martial the men. Captain Gleed, however, informed Colonel Davis that he could not willingly court martial the pilots because he felt acrobatics were good practice and useful to combat pilots. Shortly after this reply Captain Gleed was relieved of his command and assigned to the North African Ferry command as a test pilot. When this assignment was completed, Gleed returned to the group and was appointed by Colonel Davis to one of the highest positions in the group, Group Operations Officer.

Captain Pruitt completed seventy combat missions before returning to the States. He was credited with three aerial victories and shared in the sinking of an enemy destroyer. For this he was awarded the Distinguished Flying Cross and the Air Medal with six oak leaf clusters. Upon his return to the United States he was also honored by the Mayor of his home town who proclaimed December 12, 1944, "Captain Wendell O. Pruitt Day."

Death overtook Pruitt on Sunday afternoon, April 20, 1945, when his trainer plane crashed a few miles from Tuskegee Army Air Base. Although most of his comrades had witnessed many pilots meet the same fate they could hardly believe that this had happened to Pruitt. The only conclusion they could draw was that Pvt. Edward N. Thompson of Miami, Florida, who was also killed, became nervous and froze the stick when Pruitt attempted a slow roll on deck.

A Father Andrews, who officiated at Pruitt's funeral, gave a fitting epitaph of this hero when he remarked: "Captain Pruitt is dead, but the fruits of his life will be multiplied over the earth. He was a student; a man who used his intellectual abilities to achieve. All of us could learn from Wendell Pruitt the necessity of labor to accomplish our goal. We knew him as an interesting and unassuming young man, daring but not bold; vigorous and energetic, but not offensive; a good citizen, a good friend, and a devout Catholic. We needed a modern hero for us to pattern our lives so God called him home."

Andrew D. Turner

When it became known that Negroes were to be accepted for pilot training air minded youths throughout the United States rushed to make application. One of such men was Andrew D. Turner of Washington, D. C. "Jug", as he was known by his comrades, was born in Washington, D. C., on January 6, 1920. After completing his elementary training at Deanwood Elementary School he entered Dunbar High School in Washington, D. C. Here he began to manifest the leadership ability which he carried into military service. Upon graduation from Dunbar his classmates inserted the following poem in the class year book which most nearly described this youth:

"He stands for truth and high ideals,
Great power does he wield.
His versatility reveals
He's good in any field."

Turner was commissioned at Tuskegee Army Air Field on October 9, 1942. In March, 1943, he was transferred to Selfridge Field, Michigan, and assigned to the 100th Fighter Squadron of the 332nd Fighter Group. In July, 1943, he was

[179]

appointed operation officer of his squadron, a position he held until July 23, 1944. On this date he was appointed Commanding Officer of the 100th Squadron, succeeding Captain Robert Tresville, who failed to return from a mission.

Major Turner completed sixty-nine combat missions during his overseas service. In recognition of his outstanding achievement in aerial combat against the enemy in the North African and Mediterranean Theatres, he was awarded the Distinguished Flying Cross on July 10, 1944. He was also awarded the Air Medal with four oak leaf clusters and a certificate of valor by the Commanding General of the 15th Air Force. As a member of the 332nd Fighter Group he was also awarded the Presidential Unit Citation. He was also credited with participating in seven campaigns which included the Rome Arno, Southern France, Northern France, Balkans, Germany, the Apennines, and the Po Valley.

At the conclusion of the European War, Major Turner volunteered to assist Colonel Davis in leading the 477th Composite Group into combat against the Japs. He returned to the United States on June 10, 1945, and reported for duty as Deputy Group Commander of the 477th Composite Group on July 17, 1945.

The war with Japan terminated before the group could be sent into action against the Japs. However, he remained at Godman Field and moved with the 477th Composite Group to its new home at Lockbourne Army Air Base in Columbus, Ohio, on March 13, 1946.

On May 1, 1946, the 477th Composite Group was reorganized into the 332nd Fighter Group. The 100th Fighter Squadron was reactivated and Major Turner was again appointed its leader. A few months later, on August 15, the group was reorganized into the 332nd Fighter Wing and Major Turner was appointed Operation and Training Officer. Like numerous combat pilots, Major Turner fought throughout the war without a serious accident only to lose his life on a routine training flight. On September 18, 1947, Major Turner's plane collided in mid air with a plane piloted by Lieut. Milton Hall of Kentucky. Both pilots were killed. Thus ended the career of one of the most outstanding leaders of the 332nd Fighter Group.

Lee Rayford

One of the most decorated Negro pilots of the United States Army Air Force is Major Lee Rayford of Ardwick, Maryland. Rayford was born in April, 1918, in West Chester, Pennsylvania, and was enrolled in the graduate school at Howard University when the war began. On September 30, 1941, he enlisted in the Air Corps and was commissioned as a second lieutenant on May 20, 1942. Rayford was sent overseas with the 99th Fighter Squadron. Upon the completion of his tour of duty, he returned to the States. He was reassigned to the 332nd Fighter Group and appointed Operation Officer of the 301st Fighter Squadron. Shortly after the group was sent into combat Rayford was elevated to the command of the 301st Squadron. He completed ninety missions in his two tours of combat. For his outstanding service he was awarded the Distinguished Flying Cross, the Air Medal with six oak leaf clusters, the Purple Heart, the Order of Yugoslavia Partisans Red Star, the American Defense Medal, and the Victory Medal.

Edward C. Gleed

On the afternoon of November 25, 1942, a tall, slender cadet stood beside a fighter plane on the runway at Tuskegee. As he listened attentively to an instructor, a large gathering of spectators formed on the edge of the runway to watch what was to be the first attempt of a Negro to fly the P-39 Aerocobra. This plane differed from the conventional fighter plane in that it had tricycle landing gears.

For an hour the instructor went over the procedures of flying the plane with the young cadet. Then the cadet climbed into the plane and started the engine. A few minutes later the plane raced down the runway and an outburst of applause went up from the spectators as the plane rose swiftly into the air.

The young pilot maneuvered his ship over the field for

[181]

forty minutes. Then he pointed his spiral-nosed plane towards the ground and came in for a landing. In his first attempt to land, he overshot the runway. He circled the field and tried a second landing. This time he made a perfect three-point landing. The cadet who flew this historic mission was Edward C. Gleed.

Gleed was born and reared in Lawrence, Kansas. Upon the completion of high school, he enrolled at the University of Kansas. Here he successfully completed his studies. With the ambition to become a lawyer he entered Howard University Law School. By this time the war was in full force. Unable to place his personal ambition above his country, he left school and enlisted with the 9th Cavalry, which was then stationed at Fort Riley, Kansas. His knowledge of law brought him back to Washington, D. C., where he was assigned to the Military Intelligence Department. The desire for action and excitement would not let him be satisfied with this assignment. He made application for pilot training and was sent to Tuskegee for training. Here he almost immediately showed aptitude and ability to fly. When the Air Force decided to test the ability of Negroes to fly the new P-39 Aerocobra, Gleed as a cadet was chosen to make the experimental flight. After graduating as a second lieutenant he was assigned to the 332nd Fighter Group. Later he was appointed as Squadron Commander of the 301st Fighter Squadron. Shortly after entering combat, and upon the request of General Strother of the 15th Air Force, he was relieved of his command and sent on detached service to North Africa as a test pilot. Upon his return to the 332nd Fighter Group, he was appointed Group Operation Officer. This position he held until he returned to the United States at the conclusion of the war in Europe.

Gleed, like many of his comrades, could not remain idle. He volunteered for more combat service and was assigned as Operation Officer of the 477th Composite Group, which was scheduled to fight the Japs. However, the war in the Pacific ended before the 477th could be sent overseas. In March, 1946, the 477th Composite Group was moved to Lockbourne Air Field in Columbus, Ohio. Here the group was reorganized as the 332nd Fighter Group and later as the 332nd Fighter Wing. Gleed maintained his position as operation officer in the new organizations and served efficiently until the 332nd was deactivated in July 1949.

Robert B. Tresville ✳

The early death of Captain Robert B. Tresville perhaps robbed the 332nd of one of its most promising leaders. Captain Tresville was born on May 9, 1921, at the Station Hospital, Fort Huachuca, Arizona, where his father, an army band leader, was at the time stationed. Shortly after Tresville's birth his father was transferred to Fort Bennings, Georgia, where he became director of the famous 24th Infantry band.

From the time he was old enough to stand alone and go with his father to look at the big guns at Fort Bennings, young Tresville's every move was in the direction of a military career. He had hardly finished elementary school at Columbus, Georgia, when his father sent him to Germantown, Pennsylvania, to enter high school. He was graduated from high school in 1938 with honors and entered Pennsylvania State College in September, 1938. After spending one year at Pennsylvania State he was appointed by Congressman Arthur Mitchell to the United States Military Academy at West Point.

While at West Point Tresville applied for pilot training. He was sent to Tuskegee Army Air Field, where he won his wings in January, 1943. Upon receiving his wings he went back to West Point and received his commission as Second Lieutenant in the regular Army of the United States.

When the 332nd Fighter Group went overseas in January, 1944, Captain Tresville was sent with the Group as Commanding Officer of the 100th Fighter Squadron. Before he was reported missing on June 24, 1944, Tresville had completed twenty-three missions, and on each he displayed leadership and courage which won the admiration of all who flew with him.

[183]

CHAPTER XXIV

THE UNSUNG HEROES

Even the most versatile writer would find it impossible to relate adequately the part played by all the members of any particular outfit. There are almost as many stories of bravery as there are pilots in a combat organization. Yet the fact that most of these stories will never be written is no indication that the pilots who made these stories were not as important to the success of their outfits as those who received the publicity. Many of these men were the backbone of their organizations and were considered by their comrades as the most capable and dependable pilots of their outfits. Unfortunately, however, these men failed to register popular victories and as a result received little recognition outside their outfits.

Willie Fuller

The highly popular victory of the Air Force in conquering the island of Pantelleria without the use of the ground forces is one of the highlights of World War II. It was the first time in history that the Air Force had completely subdued a territory. The battle of Pantelleria had still another highlight. It was the first time Negro airmen fought against the enemy. Although the 99th as a squadron was credited with playing a significant role in subduing the island, little is known of the individual pilots whose bravery brought the Squadron success in its first campaign. One of these pilots was Lieut. Willie Fuller. Fuller was born on August 2, 1919, in Tarboro, North Carolina. After completing high school in Tarboro, he enrolled at Tuskegee Institute. He was a student there when construction began on the new Tuskegee Army Air Base. Thrilled over the new opportunity offered to Negro youths, he applied for cadet training. He was accepted as a cadet and on August 5, 1942, was commissioned and assigned to the 99th Fighter Squadron. In April, 1943, he was sent overseas. He completed over seventy missions before returning to the States.

Walter I. Lawson

Lieut. Walter Lawson was another pioneer of the 99th Fighter Squadron who received very little credit for the part he played in carrying the battle to the enemy. Lawson was born in Chancellor, Virginia, on November 7, 1919. He attended Hampton Institute in Hampton, Virginia, for three years and a half before entering the Air Corps on November 23, 1941. He was sent to Tuskegee where he won his wings on August 5, 1942. Lawson was sent overseas with the first group of pilots of the 99th Squadron. In combat he distinguished himself as one of the most aggressive and daring pilots.

James T. Wiley

There was also among the first group of replacements for the 99th, a young and unusually neat fellow whose reticent and dignified manner caused his friends to nickname him "The Little Flower." This young pilot, James T. Wiley, hailed from Pittsburgh, Pennsylvania. Wiley was actually born in Bransville, Indiana, on August 2, 1918, but claimed Pittsburgh as his home when he matriculated at the University of Pittsburgh. He was awarded a Bachelor of Arts degree from the school in 1940. He entered Carnegie Institute of Technology following his graduation and was a student there when he was accepted as an Air Corps cadet on February 2, 1942. Wiley was commissioned at Tuskegee Army Air Field on July 3, 1942. On April 16, 1943, Wiley—together with four other replacement pilots, Lieuts. Clinton B. Mills, Edward Toppins, John Morgan, and John Gibson—arrived overseas and joined the 99th Fighter Squadron. Wiley was one of the five pilots selected by Colonel Davis to make the initial flight of the 99th against the enemy. He completed eighty-five missions before returning to the States on May 31, 1944.

Once back in the States, Wiley was reassigned to Tuskegee Army Air Base. Here he was made a cadet instructor. Because

[185]

his experience as a combat pilot made him more valuable to the 477th Bomber Group, an all Negro group scheduled for combat in the Pacific, Wiley was later sent to Douglas Field, Arizona, and given transition training as a bomber pilot. When this training was finished he was sent to Godman Field, Kentucky, where he joined the 477th Group. The war in the Pacific ended before the 477th could be sent overseas and Wiley lost the chance to engage the Japs in combat.

Louis R. Purnell

There were few pilots of the 99th Fighter Squadron and the 332nd Fighter Group who saw more combat duty than Captain Louis R. Purnell of Snow Hill, Maryland. Purnell studied for three years at Lincoln University in Pennsylvania before enlisting as a cadet in the Air Corps. He was commissioned at Tuskegee on July 3, 1942, and assigned to the 99th Fighter Squadron. Purnell was sent overseas with the 99th and fought four months before being sent back to the States to join the 332nd Fighter Group which was about to make its debut in combat. Upon joining the 332nd, he was given the administrative position of Assistant Group Operations Officer. Administrative duty, however, did not appeal to Purnell and shortly after the Group entered combat he requested flying duty. His request was granted and he returned to combat flying. He completed eighty-eight missions with the 12th and 15th Air Forces. For his outstanding bravery and devotion to duty he was awarded the Distinguished Flying Cross and the Air Medal with eight oak leaf clusters.

Alva Temple

The 332nd Fighter Group, like the 99th Fighter Squadron, had many pilots who did not receive the publicity they merited. One of these pilots was Captain Alva Temple of Carrollton, Alabama. Temple, a slender, raw-boned youth, was perhaps the quietest member of the group. Temple loved to fly and was always willing to make a mission though he realized the risk involved. In combat, Temple flew most of the time as wingman for Captain Edward Toppins, one of the group's most aggressive and popular pilots. This gave Temple very little opportunity to shoot at enemy aircraft. In spite of this Temple won respect as a very competent pilot. Whereas Toppins was colorful, aggressive, and daring, Temple was reliable, dependable, and unexcitable. He gave Toppins the confidence that he was invulnerable in attacks from the rear. This confidence enabled Toppins to take chances that he otherwise would have been hesitant to take, and as a result Toppins scored several aerial victories.

Heber Houston

Like Captain Temple, Lieut. Heber Houston of Detroit, Michigan, was also a very dependable pilot. Houston entered combat with the 99th Fighter Squadron in the early part of the war and flew over seventy-five missions before returning to the States. Though he received little popularity outside his own outfit, there was no question as to his bravery and ability as a fighter pilot. For example, in three days of fighting over the Anzio beachhead he was forced to hitch hike back to the base two times. On the first day his carburetor went bad. This forced him to belly land on an emergency strip. The following day his plane again developed engine trouble and again, rather than lose his ship, he belly landed in a field. In spite of his bravery, however, Houston returned to the States and was received as just another pilot.

Alton F. Ballard

As a leader, Captain Alton F. Ballard was excelled by very few members of the 332nd Fighter Group. Ballard was born in Pasadena, California. He attended elementary and high school in that city and was a junior at Santa Barbara State College when the United States declared war on Germany.

Ballard was accepted as an aviation cadet in April, 1942, and was sent to Tuskegee where he won his wings on April 30, 1943. He was assigned to the 301st in January, 1944, and was sent overseas.

In combat Ballard displayed leadership that brought him promotions to First Lieutenant in July, 1944, and Captain in

January, 1945. He flew eighty-nine missions over Italy, France, Hungary, Yugoslavia, Greece, Romania, and Germany. He was awarded the Distinguished Flying Cross, the Air Medal, and the E. T. O. Ribbon.

Wilson Eagleson

In the early part of the war, when the 99th Fighter Squadron was being highly criticized for its failure to shoot down enemy aircraft, there arrived overseas a group of eager replacement pilots who boasted they would show the older members of the Squadron how to shoot down enemy aircraft. Naturally these arrogant newcomers antagonized the older members of the 99th. The older members, however, were quite willing to wait and watch this cockiness get knocked out of these "eager beavers" by the rigors of combat.

Among this group of replacements was a soft spoken but loquacious pilot who seemed more arrogant than the others. He had come overseas to shoot down enemy aircraft and nothing would stop him. This young pilot was Lieut. Wilson V. Eagleson of Bloomington, Indiana.

Only seven days passed before Eagleson's ability as a combat pilot was put to a test. On the afternoon of January 27, 1944, he was flying as a wingman for Captain Erwin Lawrence, Jr., of Cleveland, Ohio, when a flight of enemy planes was sighted over the Anzio beachhead. In the battle that followed, Lieut. Eagleson scored his first victory. In relating the mission, Eagleson said: "It was about my fifth mission. The mission was to Anzio Beachhead. At that time the 99th was attached to the 79th Fighter Group. For over a period of nine months the Squadron had been on strafing duty, but had never encountered enemy aircraft. Each day it seemed that the Germans would bomb between missions. That is, as soon as the 99th would leave an area, the Germans would come in and bomb. On this particular mission we were late arriving over the target. We arrived in time, however, to observe the Germans making their run in to bomb. We were flying P-40s and realized that we could not head off the Germans who were flying much faster planes. We decided to stay up about ten thousand feet and wait until the Germans finished bombing, then as they pulled up out of their dives we pounced upon them. This we did, and when the time came for us to make our attack I followed Captain Lawrence. However, Captain Lawrence was so eager to make the kill he overshot the aircraft he selected to attack. The enemy fell in behind Lawrence and opened fire on him. But while the enemy pilot was busy trying to shoot Captain Lawrence down I pulled up behind him and began to fire. After a few bursts the enemy plane began to smoke. A few more bursts caused it to fall off and head down to the ground. I followed the falling plane and continued to fire on it until it was hardly one hundred feet above the ground."

A week later on February 7, 1944, Lieut. Eagleson scored another victory for the 99th Fighter Squadron. Three Focke Wulf 190s were sighted by his flight on a patrol mission over the Anzio area. This patrol consisted of Captain Leonard Jackson of Fort Worth, Texas, Lieuts. Clinton B. Mills of Durham, North Carolina, Bernard Knighten of Tulsa, Oklahoma, and Eagleson. The Germans attempted to flee, but Eagleson and his comrades were not to be denied victories. In spite of their comparatively slow planes they gave chase and destroyed the entire group of enemy aircraft.

Harry A. Sheppard

When the War Department announced that it was accepting Negro youths in the Air Force, Harry A. Sheppard was one of the first to volunteer. Sheppard was born in New York City on October 24, 1917. He enrolled in the school of Technology at City College following his graduation from Jamaica High School. He abandoned his studies in electrical engineering to enlist in the Air Force on April 1, 1944. Sheppard was sent to Chanute Field Air Force Technical School for mechanic training. Upon completion of his training as a mechanic, he was sent to Tuskegee with the first group of enlisted men assigned to the 99th Fighter Squadron. Sheppard was not satisfied with being just a mechanic. He applied for pilot training and was

[189]

accepted as a cadet in October, 1942. On May 28, 1943, he was commissioned and assigned to the 302nd Fighter Squadron which was then stationed at Oscoda, Michigan. In January, 1944, he was sent overseas with the 332nd Fighter Group. He flew eighty-seven missions with the 12th Tactical Air Force and thirty-six missions with the 15th Strategic Air Force before returning to the United States. Sheppard not only did his share in combat flying but served as Engineering and Technical Supply Officer for the 332nd Group as well. For his outstanding services in combat he was awarded the Distinguished Flying Cross and the Air Medal with oak leaf clusters.

Gordon M. Rapier

Captain Gordon Rapier was born in Chicago, Illinois, but his family moved to Gary, Indiana, when he was very young. He was a student at the University of Chicago when the war began. He enlisted in the Army at Fort Wayne, Indiana, on December 14, 1942, and was commissioned at Tuskegee on March 12, 1944. Rapier joined the 301st Fighter Squadron in Rametelli, Italy on August 14, 1944, and flew sixty missions before returning to the States in October 1945. Rapier was awarded the Air Medal with five clusters, the Distinguished Flying Cross, and the Unit Citation Ribbon.

Charles F. Jamerson

Charles F. Jamerson was born in Louisiana, but moved to California at an early age. After completing High School, he entered San Jose State College and was an engineering student when the war began. He enlisted in the Air Force at March Field on April 1, 1941, and was sent to Tuskegee. On March 25, 1943, he was commissioned and assigned to the 332nd Fighter Group. Jamerson was sent overseas with the 332nd in January, 1944, and was assigned to the 99th Fighter Squadron. He flew seventy-eight missions with the 99th and was credited with damaging a jet plane in a running battle in which he chased the German aircraft within ten minutes of Berlin.

Leonard F. Turner

Lieut. Leonard F. Turner was also one of the many unfortunate pilots who fought gallantly as a member of the 332nd Fighter Group but received little publicity because he failed to register an aerial victory. Turner was born in Washington, D. C. After graduating from Dunbar High School he enrolled at Howard University. He entered cadet training in June, 1942, and was graduated on June 30, 1943. Upon receiving his commission he was assigned to the 301st Fighter Squadron and sent overseas with the 332nd Group. Turner flew seventy missions before returning to the States in December, 1944. He was awarded the Distinguished Flying Cross, the Air Medal with four oak leaf clusters, and the European Campaign Ribbon with four battle stars.

John H. Leahr

Leahr was born in Cincinnati, Ohio. He attended Wilberforce University two years, then transferred to the University of Cincinnati. But the desire to fly forced him to leave school and make application for pilot training. On July 28, 1943, Leahr was commissioned at Tuskegee Army Air Field as a Fighter Pilot and assigned to the 301st Fighter Squadron of the 332nd Fighter Group. He was sent overseas with the 332nd in January, 1944, and flew seventy-two missions before returning to the States on January 25, 1945.

Lowell C. Steward

Captain Lowell C. Steward was one of the most loquacious and "happy-go-lucky" pilots of the 332nd Fighter Group. But the fact that he was awarded the Distinguished Flying Cross, the E. T. O. Ribbon with four battle stars, and the Air Medal with four oak leaf clusters is ample proof that he took his flying seriously. Steward was born in Los Angeles, California. He attended school in Los Angeles and was graduated from college with a Bachelor of Arts degree in Physical Education. On July 28, 1943, Steward was commissioned as a Second Lieutenant in the Air Corps at Tuskegee Army Air Base and assigned to the 100th Fighter Squadron of the 332nd Fighter

[191]

Group. He entered combat with the Group in January, 1944, and completed forty-six missions. He returned to the States in March, 1946, and was reassigned to Tuskegee Army Air Field as a cadet instructor.

APPENDIX

COMBAT RECORD OF NEGRO AIRMEN
June 9, 1945

	DESTROYED	DAMAGED	TOTAL
Aircraft (aerial)	111	25	136
Aircraft (ground)	150	123	273
Barges and Boats	16	24	40
Box cars, Other Rolling Stock	58	561	619
Buildings & Factories	0	23	23
Gun Emplacements	3	0	3
Destroyers	1	0	1
Horse Drawn Vehicles	15	100	115
Motor Transports	6	81	87
Power Transformers	3	2	5
Locomotives	57	69	126
Radar Installations	1	8	9
Tanks on Flat Cars	0	7	7
Oil and Ammunition Dumps	2	0	2
Total Missions 12th Air Force			1267
Total Missions 15th Air Force			311
Total Sorties 12th Air Force			6381
Total Sorties 15th Air Force			9152
Grand Total Missions			1578
Grand Total Sorties			15533
Total number of pilots sent overseas			450
Total number of pilots graduated at Tuskegee			992
Awards:			
Legion of Merit			1
Silver Star			1
Soldier Medal			2

Purple Heart	8
Distinguished Flying Cross	95
Bronze Star	14
Air Medal and Clusters	744

*Final total of Distinguished Flying Crosses awarded
to Negro pilots estimated at: 150

RECORD OF ENEMY AIRCRAFT SHOT DOWN
BY NEGRO PILOTS

1. Lieut. Clarence W. Allen, Mobile, Alabama—1 FW 190 shared with Capt. Baugh (Jan. 28, 1944)
2. Capt. Lee Archer, New York City—1 ME 109 (July 18, 1944); 1 ME 109 (July 20, 1944); 3 ME 109s (Oct. 13, 1944)
3. Lieut. Willie Ashley, Sumter, S. C.—1 FW 190 (Jan. 27, 1944)
4. Lieut. Charles Bailey, Punta Gorda, Florida—1 FW 190 Jan. 27, 1944); 1 FW 190 (July 18, 1944)
5. Capt. Howard L. Baugh, Petersburg, Va.—1 FW 190 shared with Lieut. Allen (Jan. 28, 1944)
6. Lieut. Rual W. Bell, Portland, Oregon—1 FW 190 (March 31, 1945)
7. F/O Charles V. Brantley, St. Louis, Missouri—1 Jet ME 262 (March 24, 1945)
8. Lieut. Thomas P. Braswell, Buford, Georgia—1 FW 190
9. Capt. Roscoe Browne, New York City—1 Jet ME 262 (March 24, 1945)
10. Lieut. John F. Briggs, St. Louis, Missouri—1 ME 109 (August 24, 1944)
11. Capt. Charles M. Bussey, Los Angeles, California—1 ME 109 (June 9, 1944)
12. Lieut. Col. William A. Campbell, Tuskegee Institute, Alabama—2 ME 109s (March 31, 1945)

[194]

13. Lieut. Earl Carey, St. Louis, Missouri—2 ME 109s (April 1, 1945)
14. Capt. Lemuel R. Custis, Hartford, Connecticut—1 Macchi 205 (Jan. 27, 1944)
15. Capt. Alfonso W. Davis, Omaha, Nebraska—1 Macchi 205 (July 16, 1944)
16. Lieut. John W. Davis, Kansas City, Kansas—1 ME 109
17. Lieut. Robert Diez, Portland, Oregon—1 FW 190 (Jan. 27, 1944); 1 FW 190 (Jan. 28, 1944)
18. Capt. Elwood T. Driver, Trenton, New Jersey—1 FW 190 (Feb. 5, 1944)
19. Lieut. Wilson V. Eagleson, Bloomington, Indiana—1 FW 190 (Jan. 27, 1944); 1 FW 190 (July 20, 1944)
20. Lieut. John E. Edwards, Steubenville, Ohio—2 ME 109s (April 1, 1945)
21. Capt. Joseph D. Elsberry, Langston, Oklahoma—3 FW 190s (July 12, 1944); 1 FW 190 (July 20, 1944)
22. F/O James Fischer, Stoughton, Massachusetts—1 ME 109 (April 1, 1945)
23. Lieut. Frederick Funderburg, Monticello, Georgia—2 ME 109s (June 9, 1944)
24. Major Edward C. Gleed, Lawrence, Kansas—2 FW 190s (July 27, 1944)
25. Lieut. William W. Green, Staunton, Virginia—1 Macchi 205 (July 16, 1944); 1 ME 109 (July 26, 1944 shared with Lieut. Groves); 1 ME 109 (Oct. 13, 1944)
26. Capt. Claude B. Govan, Newark, New Jersey—1 ME 109 (July 27, 1944)
27. Lieut. Alfred N. Gorham, Waukiska, Washington—2 FW 190s (July 27, 1944)
28. Lieut. Weldon Groves, Edwardsville, Kansas—1 ME 109 (July 26, 1944 shared with Lieut. Green)
29. Capt. George Gray, Welch, West Virginia—1 ME 109 (Oct. 4, 1944)
30. Capt. Charles B. Hall, Brazil, Indiana—1 FW 190 (July 2, 1943); 1 FW 190 and 1 ME 109 (Jan. 28, 1944)

31. Lieut. James L. Hall, Jr., Washington, D. C.—1 ME 109
32. Lieut. Richard W. Hall, Albany, Georgia—1 ME 109 (July 27, 1944)
33. Lieut. Milton Hayes, Los Angeles, California—1 ME 109 (Oct. 4, 1944 shared with Capt. Perry)
34. Lieut. Jack Holsclaw, Spokane, Washington—2 ME 109s (July 18, 1944)
35. Lieut. William Hill—1 ME 109 (August 23, 1944)
36. Capt. Freddie Hutchins, Donaldsonville, Georgia—1 ME 109 (July 26, 1944)
37. Lieut. Thomas W. Jefferson, Chicago, Illinois—2 ME 109s (April 26, 1945)
38. Capt. Melvin T. Jackson, Warrenton, Virginia—1 ME 109 (June 9, 1944)
39. Capt. Leonard M. Jackson, Fort Worth, Texas—1 FW 190 (Feb. 7, 1944); 1 ME 109 (July 26, 1944); 1 ME 109 (July 27, 1944)
40. Lieut. Carl E. Johnson, Charlottesville, Virginia—1 ME 109 (August 6, 1944); 1 Reggiane 2001 (July 30, 1944)
41. Lieut. Langdon E. Johnson, Ramp, West Virginia—1 ME 109 (July 20, 1944)
42. Lieut. Felix Kirkpatrick, Jr., Chicago, Illinois—1 ME 109 (July 27, 1944)
43. Lieut. Earle R. Lane, Wickliffe, Ohio—1 Jet ME 262 (March 24, 1945)
44. Lieut. Jimmie Lanham, Philadelphia, Pennsylvania—1 ME 109 and 1 Probable (April 26, 1944)
45. Capt. Clarence Lester, Chicago, Illinois—3 ME 109s (July 18, 1944)
46. F/O John H. Lyle, Chicago, Illinois—1 ME 109 (March 31, 1944)
47. Lieut. Walter Manning, Philadelphia, Pennsylvania—1 ME 109 (April 1, 1945)
48. Capt. Armour G. McDaniel, Martinsville, Virginia—1 ME 109 (July 20, 1944)

49. Capt. Charles E. McGee, Champaign, Illinois—1 ME 109 (Oct. 4, 1944)
50. Lieut. Clinton B. Mills, Durham, North Carolina—1 FW 190 (Feb. 7, 1944)
51. Lieut. Harold Morris, Portland, Oregon—1 ME 109 (April 1, 1945)
52. Capt. Walter J. Palmer, New York City—1 ME 109 (July 18, 1944)
53. Capt. Henry Perry, Thomasville, Georgia—1 ME 109 (Oct. 4, 1944 shared with Lieut. Milton Hayes, Los Angeles, California)
54. Lieut. William S. Price, Topeka, Kansas—1 ME 109 (Feb. 1, 1945)
55. Capt. Wendell O. Pruitt, St. Louis, Missouri—1 ME 109 (June 9, 1944); 2 ME 109s (Oct. 12, 1944)
56. Lieut. George M. Rhodes, Brooklyn, New York—1 FW 190 (August 12, 1944); 1 ME 109 (Oct. 4, 1944)
57. Lieut. Daniel L. Rich, Rutherford, New Jersey—1 ME 109 (March 31, 1945)
58. Capt. Leon C. Roberts, Pritchard, Alabama—1 FW 190 (Jan. 27, 1944)
59. Lieut. Roger Romine, Oakland, California—1 ME 109 (July 18, 1944); 1 ME 109 (July 26, 1944); 1 ME 109 (Oct. 13, 1944)
60. Lieut. Richard A. Simons, White Plains, New York—1 ME 109 (April 26, 1945)
61. Capt. Lewis C. Smith, Los Angeles, California—1 ME 109 (Jan. 27, 1944)
62. Lieut. Luther H. Smith, Jr., Des Moines, Iowa—1 ME 109 (July 17, 1944); 1 ME 109 (Oct. 13, 1944)
63. Lieut. Robert Smith, Baltimore, Maryland—1 ME 109 (July 17, 1944)
64. Lieut. Harry T. Stewart, Jr., Corona, Long Island—3 ME 109s (April 1, 1945)
65. Capt. Edward Thomas, Chicago, Illinois—1 ME 109 (Oct. 4, 1944)

66. Lieut. William H. Thomas, Los Angeles, California—1 ME 109 (August 24, 1944)
67. Capt. Edward L. Toppins, San Francisco, California—1 FW 190 (Jan. 27, 1944); 1 FW 190 (July 18, 1944); 1 ME 109 (July 20, 1944); 1 ME 109 (July 26, 1944)
68. Lieut. Hugh Warner, New York City—1 ME 109 (July 18, 1944)
69. Capt. Luke Weathers, Memphis, Tennessee—1 ME 109 (August 23, 1944 shared with Lieut. William Hill); 2 ME 109s (Nov. 16, 1944)
70. Lieut. Shelby E. Westbrook, Toledo, Ohio—1 ME 109 (Oct. 4, 1944)
71. Capt. Charles White, Oakland, California—1 ME 109 (April 1, 1945)
72. Capt. Hugh J. White, St. Louis, Missouri—1 ME 109 (March 31, 1945)
73. Lieut. Lawrence D. Wilkens, Los Angeles, California—1 ME 109 (July 17, 1944)
74. Lieut. Bertram W. Wilson, Brooklyn, New York—1 FW 190 (March 31, 1945)
75. Lieut. Robert W. Williams, Ottumwa, Iowa—2 FW 190s (March 31, 1945)

Destroyer

Lieut. Gwynne Pierson, Oakland, Calif.
Capt. Wendell O. Pruitt, St. Louis, Mo.

Shared honor of destroying a Nazi Destroyer on July 25, 1944

PILOTS AWARDED THE DISTINGUISHED FLYING CROSS

Unofficial List

Col. Benjamin O. Davis, Jr., 1721 S. Street N. W., Wash., D. C.
Major George S. Roberts, 317 Quarry Ave., Fairmount, W. Va.
Major Lee Rayford, 1822 9th Street, N. W., Wash., D. C.
Capt. Edward C. Gleed, 1721 Ohio Street, Lawrence, Kansas

Capt. Jack D. Holsclaw, 2301 W. College Ave., Spokane, Wash.

Capt. Arnold W. Cisco, 1129 Highland Ave., Alton, Illinois

Capt. Joseph D. Elsberry, 1114 N. Washington, Langston, Okla.

Capt. Claude E. Govan, 142 Somerset St., Newark, New Jersey

Capt. Harold E. Sawyers, 1587 North Star, Columbus, Ohio

Capt. Andrew D. Turner, 1000 Westford Place, N. E. Wash., D. C.

Major William T. Mattison, 2616 Park Place, N. W. Wash., D. C.

Capt. Woodrow W. Crockett, 613½ Vine Street, Little Rock, Arkansas

Capt. Lawrence E. Dickson, 220 W. 11th St., New York City

Capt. Samuel L. Curtis, 188 Fairview Ave., Yeadon, Pa.

Capt. Lowell C. Steward, 1407 E. Wash., Los Angeles, Calif.

Capt. Clarence W. Dart, Jr., 506 Dewitt Ave., Elmira, N. J.

Capt. Elwood T. Driver, 30 Fountain Ave., Trenton, N. J.

Capt. Alton F. Ballard, 372 E. Orange Grove Ave., Pasadena, Calif.

Lieut. Felix J. Kirkpatrick, Jr., 4155 Prairie Ave., Chicago, Ill.

Lieut. Richard Harder, 137 Renwich Place, Syracuse, N. Y.

Lieut. Milton S. Hayes, 377½ La Salle Ave., Los Angeles, Calif.

Lieut. Edward M. Thomas, 1245 W. 107th Place, Chicago, Ill.

Lieut. Charles W. Tate, 1004 Decatur, Pittsburgh, Pa.

Lieut. Herman A. Lawson, 204 White's Bridge, Fresno, Calif.

Lieut. Lawrence D. Wilkens, 1355 E. 53rd St., Los Angeles, Calif.

Lieut. Roger Romine, 829 36th St., Oakland, Calif.

Lieut. Luther H. Smith, Jr., Des Moines, Iowa

Lieut. William H. Thomas, 143½ W. 6th St., Los Angeles, Calif.

Lieut. Felix J. Kirkpatrick, Jr., 4155 Prairie Ave., hicago, Ill.

Lieut. William W. Green, Jr., 29 Park Boulevard, Staunton, Va.

Lieut. Lee A. Archer, Jr., 350 W. 119th St., New York City

Lieut. Frank E. Roberts, 94 Harrison St., Boston, Mass.

Lieut. George M. Rhodes, Jr., 331 Jefferson Ave., Brooklyn, N. Y.

Capt. Clarence D. Lester, 5321 Prairie Ave., Chicago, Ill.
Capt. Melvin T. Jackson, Warrenton, Va.
Capt. Vernon V. Haywood, 902 Manley St., Raleigh, N. C.
Capt. Dudley M. Watson, Frankfort, Kentucky
Capt. Gwynne W. Pierson, 865 45th St., Oakland, Calif.
Capt. Milton R. Brooks, 411 Harrison St., Glassport, Pa.
Capt. Luke J. Weathers, Jr., 601 South Lauderdale, Memphis, Tenn.
Capt. Freddie E. Hutchins, 208 N. Bowling St., Donaldsonville, Ga.
Capt. Charles B. Hall, 80 S. 18th St., Terre Haute, Indiana
Capt. Alfonso W. Davis, 2118 N. 29th St., Omaha, Nebr.
Capt. Edward L. Toppins, 1519 Baker St., San Francisco, Calif.
Capt. Howard L. Baugh, 93 Lee Ave., Petersburg, Va.
Capt. Louis R. Purnell, Snow Hill, Maryland
Lieut. Col. William A. Campbell, Tuskegee Institute, Alabama
Capt. George Gray, 809 McDowell St., Welch, W. Va.
Capt. Albert H. Manning, 269 Cemetery St., Spartanburg, S. C.
Capt. Wendell O. Pruitt, 4569 Garfield Ave., St. Louis, Mo.
Capt. Henry B. Perry, 519 N. Oak, Thomasville, Ga.
Capt. Alva N. Temple, Carrollton, Ala.
Capt. John Daniels, 15314 Vine Ave., Hartay, Ill.
Capt. Willard L. Woods, 1906 S. Lauderdale, Memphis, Tenn.
Lieut. Norman W. Scales, 1107 Myrtle St., Austin, Texas
Lieut. Walter J. Palmer, 3762 Park Ave., New York City
Lieut. Leonard F. Turner, 244 P St., N. W. Wash., D. C.
Lieut. Dempsey W. Morgan, Jr., 6062 Calfax, Detroit, Mich.
Lieut. Robert L. Martin, 560 Hill St., Dubuque, Iowa
Lieut. Lawrence B. Jefferson, 1029 Sigsla, Grand Rapids, Mich.
Lieut. John F. Briggs, Jr., 3651 Finney St., St. Louis, Mo.
Lieut. Spurgeon Ellington, 1302 N. Highland Ave., Winston-Salem, N. C.
Capt. Leonard M. Jackson, 1200 Missouri Ave., Ft. Worth, Texas
Capt. Robert J. Friend, Washington, D. C.
Capt. Henry R. Peoples, St. Louis, Mo.

Capt. Marion R. Rodgers, Detroit, Mich.

Capt. Charles L. White, 4278 W. St. Ferdinand Ave., St. Louis, Mo.

Lieut. Roscoe C. Browne, Jr., New York City

Lieut. Earle R. Lane, Wickliffe, Ohio

Lieut. William S. Price, Topeka, Kansas

Lieut. Charles V. Brantley, St. Louis, Mo.

Lieut. Hannibal M. Cox, Jr., 6639 S. Rhodes Ave., Chicago, Ill.

Lieut. Vincent I. Mitchell, 4468 Kentucky Ave., Mt. Clemens, Mich.

Capt. Gordon M. Rapier, 2549 Madison St., Gary, Indiana

Lieut. Thomas W. Jefferson, Chicago, Ill.

Lieut. James Lanham, Philadelphia, Pa.

Lieut. Thomas P. Braswell, Buford, Ga.

Lieut. Shelby F. Westbrook, Toledo, Ohio

Lieut. William H. Walker, Carbondale, Ill.

Lieut. John W. Davis, Kansas City, Kansas

Lieut. Quitman C. Walker, Indianola, Miss.

Lieut. Heber C. Houston, Detroit, Mich.

Lieut. Charles P. Bailey, Punta Gorda, Fla.

Capt. Walter M. Downs, McComb, Miss.

Capt. Clarence H. Bradford, St. Louis, Mo.

Lieut. Reid E. Thompson, New Rochelle, N. Y.

Lieut. Gentry E. Barnes, 307 E. Locust St., Lawrenceville, Ill.

Lieut. John E. Edwards, Steubenville, Ohio

Lieut. Robert W. William, Ottumwa, Iowa

Lieut. Bertram W. Wilson, Brooklyn, N. Y.

Lieut. Harry T. Stewart, Jr., 105-11 34th Ave., Corona, N. Y.

Capt. Emile C. Clifton, Jr., San Francisco, Calif.

Capt. Theodore A. Wilson, 47 Patton Ave., N. E., Roanoke, Va.

May 1949

"Commanding Officer
Lockbourne Air Force Base
Columbus, Ohio
Greetings:

In my capacity as Governor of Ohio and individually, I desire to commend Captain Alva Temple of the 301st Fighter Squadron, Lieutenant Harry Stewart of the 100th Fighter Squadron and Lieutenant James Harvey of the 99th Fighter Squadron, who represented the 332nd Fighter Group in the Conventional Fighter Class of the Air Force National Fighter Gunnery Meet at Las Vegas Air Force Base, Nevada.

The winning of first place in open competition by your men situated at Lockbourne Air Force Base is a source of gratification to all people of Ohio, and will serve as an inspiration, particularly to the youth of this state.

Congratulations and best wishes.

Sincerely,
Frank J. Lausche."

MAY 1949

"Capt. Alva Temple, 301st Fighter Squadron
Lt. Harry Stewart, 100th Fighter Squadron
Lt. James Harvey, 99th Fighter Squadron
Representing the 332nd Fighter Group

COMMENDATION

It is extremely gratifying to learn that the 332nd Fighter Group stationed at the Lockbourne Air Force Base won the first place in the Conventional Fighter Class of the Air Force National Fighter Gunnery Meet at Las Vegas Air Force Base, Nevada, recently. The 332nd Fighter Group is to be highly complimented on having officers of such high caliber and skill that bring renown and fame, not only to Lockbourne Air Force Base, but upon the City of Columbus and the State of Ohio as well. Truly, it is this type of achievement that is an inspiration for American youth and assurance to the people of this country of adequate protection in the event of an emergency.

Permit me as State Commander of the Air Force Association to personally commend Captain Temple, Lieutenant Stewart and Lieutenant Harvey on their great achievement.

Yours very truly,
Fred M. Pickens
State Commander, Ohio Wing
Air Force Association."

TWXs received by 332nd Headquarters: MAY 1949

From: Commanding General,
        Continental Air Command,
        Mitchell Air Force Base, N. Y.

My personal congratulations to members of the 332nd Fighter Group for taking first place in the Conventional Aircraft Class at the 1949 Annual Air Gunnery Meet held at Las Vegas Air Force Base.

*   *   *

From: Commanding General,
        9th Air Force,
        Langley Air Force Base, Va.

Congratulations to members of the 332nd Fighter Gunnery Team for splendid showing in winning first place in Conventional Division of 1949 USAF Gunnery Meet at Las Vegas Air Force Base.

Lockbourne Air Force Base,   MAY 1949
Columbus, Ohio
Subject: Letter of commendation
To: 332nd Fighter Group Detachment,
        Las Vegas Air Force Base,
        Nevada

It is with a great deal of personal pride that I commend the members of the 332nd Fighter Detachment which won the USAF Fighter Gunnery Meet for Conventional Aircraft at Las Vegas Air Force Base last week. Your team was composed of armament, maintenance, administrative, operations and pilot personnel, all of whom had to exhibit the highest type of cooperation, teamwork, and individual skill.

I add my congratulations to the many others you have received.

Benjamin O. Davis, Jr.
Colonel, USAF Commanding.

[203]

TUSKEGEE HONOR ROLL

Men Lost in Training, Combat, and on Routine Missions

F/O William P. Armstrong, 93 Codling Street, Providence, Rhode Island. Shot down April 1, 1945 over Vienna, Austria.

F/O George A. Bates, 6231 Eberhart Ave., Chicago, Illinois. Killed in plane crash at Milstead, Alabama on April 26, 1946.

Lieut. Richard H. Bell, 6535 Eberhart Ave., Chicago, Illinois. Died in training at Waterboro, Kentucky on August 10, 1944.

Lieut. Celsus E. Beguesse (MC), 910 South Walcott Ave., Chicago, Illinois. Died in plane crash at Tuskegee on May 19, 1946.

Lieut. Samuel A. Black, Plainfield, New Jersey. Bomber pilot —Died in crash at Madison, Kentucky.

Lieut. Linson Blackney, Weather Officer—Died when plane piloted by Lieut. Nathaniel Hill spun into Lake Huron on June 16, 1943.

Lieut. Fred L. Brewer, Charlotte, North Carolina. Died when his plane spun in over the Alps.

Lieut. Sidney Brooks, 3709 E. 142nd Street, Cleveland, Ohio. Killed on Aug. 19, 1943 in Sicily.

Lieut. James E. Brothers, 5336 Kenwood Ave., Chicago, Illinois. Killed at Tuskegee in plane crash in May 1943.

Pvt. Donald E. Brown, South Heren, Michigan. Died in plane crash at T.A.A.F. on May 19, 1946.

Lieut. James B. Brown, Los Angeles, California. Died on June 6, 1944 near Frosinone, Italy.

Lieut. Roger B. Brown, Glencoe, Illinois. Died on June 14, 1944 in Italy while taking transition training.

Lieut. Samuel Bruce, 319 12th Street, Seattle, Washington. Died in battle of Anzio Beachhead on January 28, 1944.

Lieut. James A. Calhoun, Bridgeport, Conn. Reported missing on strafing mission in Sept. 1944.

[204]

Lieut. John H. Chavis, 324 Tarboro Street, Raleigh, North Carolina. Spun into the Adriatic Sea.

Capt. Arnold Cisco, 6049 Eberhart Ave., Chicago, Illinois. Died in plane crash at T.A.A.F. on May 19, 1946.

Lieut. George Cisco, 1129 Highland Ave., Alton, Illinois. Died in plane crash at T.A.A.F.

Lieut. James Coleman, Jr., Detroit, Michigan. Died shortly after VE-Day while practicing dive bombing in Italy.

T/Sgt. Coleman Conley, Birmingham, Alabama. Died on May 19, 1946 at Tuskegee in a plane crash.

Lieut. Harry Jay Daniels, 1840 South Keystone Ave., Indianapolis, Indiana. Missing in action on coastal patrol on February 23, 1944.

Capt. John Daniels, Chicago, Illinois. Died on May 19, 1946 at T.A.A.F.

Lieut. Luther R. Davenport, Loving, Georgia. Died at Oneida, Tenn. in a plane crash.

Capt. Alfonso Davis, 2118 North 29th Street, Omaha, Nebr. Killed in plane crash in Italy.

Lieut. Richard Davis, Ft. Valley, Georgia. Died in plane crash at T.A.A.F. on January 30, 1943.

Cadet Richard A. Dawson, 122 Shenandoa Street, San Antonia, Texas. Died in training at T.A.A.F. on June 8, 1942.

Lieut. Charles Warren Dickerson, 26 Winthrop Ave., New Rochelle, New York. Died in plane crash at Selfridge Field, Mich.

Lieut. Othel Dickson, 1430 O'Farrel Street, San Francisco, Calif. Died in plane crash at Rametelli, Italy on June 28, 1944.

Lieut. Alwayne Dunlap, Washington, D. C. Died in battle of Anzio Beachhead.

Lieut. Jerome Edwards, 902 Main Street, Steubenville, Ohio. Died in crash at Oscoda, Mich.

Lieut. Spurgeon Ellington, 1302 N. Highland Ave., Winston-Salem, North Carolina. Died in plane crash near Atlanta, Ga. on Dec. 10, 1945.

Lieut. Maurice V. Esters, Box 17, Webster City, Iowa. Died in Italy in June 1944.

Lieut. William J. Faulkner, Nashville, Tenn. Failed to return from mission over Southeastern Austria on November 7, 1944.

Lieut. Samuel J. Foreman, Tulsa, Oklahoma. Reported missing in action over Europe.

Lieut. Frederick D. Funderburg 191 18th Ave., Monticello, Ga. Reported missing in bad weather over Linz, Austria in December 1944.

Lieut. Howard C. Gamble, Charleston, West Virginia. Reported missing over Europe.

Lieut. Morris E. Gant, Chicago, Illinois. Failed to return from mission over the Adriatic Sea. Complained of gas shortage.

Lieut. Clemenceau Givings, 100 E. Leigh Street, Richmond, Va. Killed in Italy on March 18, 1944.

Lieut. Walter S. Gladden, Providence, Rhode Island (Ground Officer). Killed at Lynchburg, Va.

Lieut. Joseph E. Gordon, Brooklyn, New York. Died in the invasion of Southern France on August 12, 1944.

F/O Robert A. Gordon, 26 South Cedar Street, Troy, Ohio. Died in plane crash at T.A.A.F. on May 19, 1946.

Lieut. Milton R. Hall, 2324 West 9th Street, Owensboro, Kentucky. Died in plane crash at Lockbourne, Ohio on Sept. 18, 1947.

Lieut. Richard W. Hall, Albany, Georgia. Died in plane crash near Atlanta, Georgia on Dec. 10, 1945.

Lieut. Maceo Harris, 18 Lattimore Court, Boston, Mass. Missing in action October 1944.

F/O Thomas L. Hawkins, Glen Ridge, New Jersey. Died March 7, 1945 in Italy.

Lieut. George Kenneth Hayes, 377½ La Salle Ave., Los Angeles, California. Died in plane crash near Birmingham, Ala. on June 12, 1944.

Lieut. Earl Highbaugh, 540 Udell Street, Indianapolis, Indiana. Collided near Foggia with plane piloted by Lieut. Ramsey.

Lieut. William E. Hill, 81 Boom Street, Narragansett, Rhode Island. Died at Oscoda, Michigan on Nov. 22, 1943.

Lieut. Nathaniel M. Hill, Washington, D. C. Spun into Lake Huron near Oscoda, Michigan on June 16, 1943.

Lieut. Wendell W. Hockaday, 300 Whitehead Ave., Norfolk, Va. Died strafing in Munich area about Feb. 25, 1945.

Lieut. Tommy Hood. Died when struck tree while strafing in Southern Germany.

Lieut. Stephen Hotesse, New York City, Died in plane crash near Madison, Kentucky.

F/O Sylvester H. Hurd, Jr., 102 138th Place, East Chicago, Illinois. Died in plane crash at Milstead, Alabama on April 26, 1946.

Lieut. Oscar D. Hutton, Jr., Chicago, Illinois. Died when his plane was hit by belly tank dropped from another plane while on mission, July 18, 1944.

Cadet Horace E. Joseph, Jamaica, New York. Died in plane crash near Tuskegee Air Base in Sept. 1943.

Lieut. Wellington G. Irving, 299 Central Ave., Belzuni, Miss. Lost in Kemton area on July 18, 1944.

Lieut. Spencer P. Isabelle, 6250 Bromley Ave., Oakland, California. Died at T.A.A.F. November 1945.

Lieut. Samuel Jefferson, 2813 Ave. M, Galveston, Texas. Died in action off coast of Corsica on June 22, 1944.

Lieut. Charles B. Johnson, 1544 North Gratz Street, Phila,, Pa. Died in action off coast of Corsica on June 22, 1944.

Lieut. Langdon E. Johnson, Rand, West Virginia. Failed to return from mission to Southern France, August 12, 1944.

Lieut. Edgar Jones, New York City. Died on March 28, 1944 in Italy.

F/O Robert M. Johnson, Pittsburgh, Pa. Killed at Waterboro, Kentucky. Collided with a B-24.

Lieut. Oscar Kenny, P. O. Box 248 Tuskegee Institute, Ala. Died in plane crash at T.A.A.F. on July 9, 1943.

Lieut. Earl Eugene King, 16 Center Street, Bessemer, Ala. Died in Martin Lake, Ala. March 24, 1943.

Lieut. Edward Laird, 3229 7th Ave., Brighton, Ala. Crashed on take off in Italy on June 28, 1944.

Lieut. Allen Lane, 205 Cherry Street, Demopolis, Ala. Died on cross-country flight from Lockbourne, Ohio.

Lieut. Carrol N. Langston, Jr., 6317 Lawrence Ave., Chicago, Illinois. Lost in Adriatic Sea on June 9, 1944.

Capt. Erwin Lawrence, Cleveland, Ohio. Died Oct. 4, 1944 on mission to Athens, Greece.

Lieut. Samuel Leftenant, Amityville, New York. Died in plane collision over Russian-held territory on April 12, 1945.

Capt. Walter I. Lawson, Chancellor, Virginia. Died in B-29 crash in Calif. in Feb. 1952.

Lieut. Wayne Leggins, 242 East College Ave., Springfield, Ohio. Died in Italy in May 1944.

Lieut. Walter P. Manning, 346 N. 42nd Street, Phila., Pa. Shot down over Vienna.

Lieut. Andrew D. Marshall, 433 Salisburg Street, Wadesboro, N. C. Missing in action over Greece in Dec. 1944.

Lieut. Otis E. Marshall, 1439 Lippert Rd., N. E., Canton, Ohio. Died in plane crash at T.A.A.F. in Nov. 1945.

Major Harold Martin, Washington, D. C. Killed near Reidsville, N. C. on March 23, 1945.

Lieut. Faythe A. McGinnis, 509 Hamp Street, Muskogee, Oklahoma. Died at Tuskegee on Sept. 12, 1942. Plane spun into Soughalachoe Creek, Ala.

Lieut. Vincent Jay Mason, 162 Taylor Street, Orange, New Jersey. Died at Selfridge Field, Michigan on March 17, 1944. Plane struck a garage and burst into flames.

Lieut. George McCrumby, 806 Twonply Street, Ft. Wayne, Texas. Failed to return to base after mission to Geata Point on Feb. 29, 1944.

Lieut. Cornelius May, Nashville, Tennessee. Died at Selfridge Field.

Lieut. James McCullin, 3701 Enright Ave., St. Louis, Mo. Died in battle of Pantelleria, July 1943.

A/C Raymond C. McEwen, 2439 Vincennes Street, Chicago, Ill. Died at T.A.A.F. Oct. 5, 1944.

Lieut. Paul Mitchell, 808 Howard Rd. S. E., Washington, D. C. Collided with Lieut. Sam Bruce, Aug. 1943.

Lieut. Frank H. Moody, 93 E. 55th Street, Los Angeles, Calif. Spun into Lake Huron, Michigan, April 1944.

Lieut. Roland W. Moody, 187 Fayeweather Street, Cambridge, Mass. Burned to death in tent in Italy when tank fell from a plane spraying the area for mosquitoes.

Lieut. John Morgan, Cartersville, Georgia. Died in Italy Jan. 2, 1944.

Lieut. Sidney Mosely, 1518 42nd Street, Norfolk, Va. Died at T.A.A.F. May 10, 1943.

Lieut. Andrew Maples, Jr., Box 403 Orange, Va. Missing over Italy June 26, 1944.

Capt. Mac Ross, Dayton, Ohio. Died in plane crash in Italy on July 12, 1944.

Lieut. Neal Nelson, Amarillo, Texas. Missing in Rome area on May 11, 1944.

Lieut. Elton H. Nightengale, Tuskegee, Ala. Missing in action on Nov. 27, 1944.

Lieut. Raymond F. Noches, Junction City, Kansas. Died on routine flight to Alabama in B-25.

Lieut. Leland H. Pennington, Rochester, New York. Failed to return from mission to Yugoslavia. Suffered with appendicitis may have been cause of death.

Lieut. Francis B. Peoples, 308 Rockspring Street, Henderson, N. C. Died at Tuskegee on April 27, 1944.

Lieut. Harvey N. Pinkney, Baltimore, Md. Died in plane collision at Lockbourne, Ohio in August 1948.

Lieut. James Polkinghorne, Pensacola, Florida. Missing in action on May 4, 1944.

Lieut. Henry Pollard, 225 Madison Street, Buffalo, New York. Crashed near the Capidachino Airbase in Italy on May 22, 1944.

Lieut. Driscoll Ponder, Chicago, Ill. Failed to return from a mission.

Lieut. John H. Prowell, Jr., Lewisburg, Alabama. Missing in action near Salerno on May 24, 1944.

Capt. Wendell O. Pruitt, 4569 Garfield Ave., St. Louis, Mo. Died in plane crash at Tuskegee in April 1945.

F/O Glen W. Pulliam (Navigator), Los Angeles, Calif. Died in plane crash at Madison, Kentucky.

Lieut. Leon Purchase, 164 West 141st Street, New York City. Killed at Selfridge Field, Michigan on Nov. 19, 1943.

Lieut. James C. Ramsey, Augusta, Georgia. Died in action near Foggia, Italy.

F/O Nathaniel Rayburg, Washington, D. C. Killed at Selfridge Field, Mich. in Dec. 1943.

Lieut. Emory Robbins, 738 Harguette Road, Chicago, Ill. Missing in action in Italy.

Lieut. Ronald Reeves, 2106 I Street, N. E., Washington, D. C. Failed to return from a mission.

Lieut. Robert C. Robinson, Asheville, N. C. Failed to return from Yugoslavia on June 10, 1944.

Lieut. Cornelius Rogers, Chicago, Ill. Missing on a mission to Yugoslavia on June 10, 1944.

Lieut. Roger Romine, 829 36th Street, Oakland, Calif. Died in plane collision in Italy on Nov. 16, 1944.

Lieut. Leon Roberts, 400 Murphy & McGee Street, Pritchard, Alabama. Died in action in Italy on July 11, 1944.

Lieut. Paul C. Simmons, Detroit, Michigan. Killed at Selfridge Field, Mich. in Dec. 1943 when plane threw a rod.

Lieut. Alfonso Simmons, Munerief Rd., Jacksonville, Fla. Died in action on March 3, 1945 in Northern Italy.

Lieut. Sidat Singh, Washington, D. C. Killed at Oscoda, Mich. on March 25, 1943.

Lieut. John S. Sloan, 2817 South 6th Street, Louisville, Kentucky. Shot down by flak on March 30, 1944 while dive bombing in the Cassino area.

Lieut. Arnett Stark, Jr., Los Angeles, Calif. Shot down by enemy plane on March 25, 1945.

F/O Charles W. Stephens, Monroeville, Alabama. Died in plane crash near Reidsville, N. C.

Lieut. Thomas C. Street, Springfield, New Jersey. Lost when plane spun into Adriatic Sea on March 23, 1945.

A/C Ross Stewart, Jr., Johnston, Pa. Killed at T.A.A.F. with Lieut. Brothers in May 1943.

Lieut. Nathaniel C. Stewart, Philadelphia, Pa. Killed at Selfridge Field, Michigan in Jan. 1944.

Lieut. Roosevelt Stigger, 346 Damon Street, Jackson, Michigan. Lost on mission over the Adriatic Sea.

Lieut. Norvell Stoudmire, 4448 Ferdinand Ave., St. Louis, Mo. Died on March 31, 1944 when plane crashed into surf a few yards from shore in Italy.

Lieut. John W. Squires, St. Louis, Missouri. Killed near Pisa, Italy while buzzing the 92nd Division shortly after VE-Day.

Pvt. Reginald V. Smith, Ahoskie, North Carolina. Killed at T.A.A.F. in plane crash.

Lieut. Elmer Taylor, Pittsburgh, Pa. Killed in Italy on June 2, 1944.

Capt. Edward M. Thomas, Chicago, Ill. Killed at T.A.A.F. on May 19, 1946.

A/C Cleodis V. Todd, Berkeley, Calif. Killed at T.A.A.F. in July 1944.

Capt. Edward Toppins, San Francisco, Calif. Reported died in plane crash in California.

Capt. Robert Tresville, 6502 Musgrove Street, Germantown, Pa. Missing in action on June 20, 1944.

Major Andrew Turner, 1000 Westford Place N. E., Washington, D. C. Killed at Lockbourne, Ohio on Sept. 18, 1947.

Pvt. Edward N. Thompson, Miami, Fla. Killed with Capt. Pruitt at T.A.A.F. on April 15, 1945.

Lieut. William Walker, Suffolk, Va. Killed at Selfridge Field, Mich. in 1943.

Lieut. Johnson C. Wells, 44 Pine Street, Buffalo, New York. Killed at Selfridge Field, Mich. in Oct. 1943.

Lieut. Walter Westmoreland, 375 Cain Street, N. E., Atlanta, Ga. Shot down strafing near Lake Balaton on Oct. 13, 1944.

Lieut. Leonard R. Willette, Belleville, New Jersey. Failed to return from mission over Germany on Sept. 22, 1944.

Lieut. Sherman White, Montgomery, Ala. Killed in Italy on July 2, 1943.

Lieut. Leroi Williams, Roanoke, Va. Killed in collision with plane piloted by Lieut. (Wild Bill) Walker in Nov. 1943.

Sgt. Eli B. Williams, 911 9th Ave., Middleton, Ohio. Died in crash Sept. 27, 1944 while flying with Lieut. Luther Cartwright. (white)

Lieut. William F. Williams, Jr., 319-E. 121 Street, Cleveland, Ohio. Missing in action on July 21, 1944.

Lieut. Robert H. Wiggins, Elmsford, New York. Killed in March 1945 on flight over the Adriatic Sea.

Lieut. Frank N. Wright, 121 Cobat Ave., Elmsford, New York Killed in March 1945 on mission over Europe.

Lieut. James W. Wright, 70 Sylvania Ave., Pittsburgh, Pa.

Lieut. Beryl Wyatt, 405 South 14th Street, Independence, Kansas. Killed in Italy on April 17, 1944.

Lieut. Albert L. Young, 590 South Wellington Street, Memphis, Tenn. Died in Italy when tried to land with an extra gas tank. Plane burst into flames.

Lieut. Carl J. Woods, Box 177 Mars, Pa. Killed in Italy.

Pvt. Euclid R. Montgomery, Chicago, Ill. Killed at T.A.A.F. on May 19, 1946.

Major William T. Mattison, Conway, Arkansas and 2616 Park Place N. W., Wash., D. C. Killed in plane crash near Toledo, Ohio on Jan. 28, 1951.

Capt. Albert Manning, 435 19th Street, N. E., Washington, D. C. and Hartsville, S. C. Killed in plane crash near Toledo, Ohio on Jan. 28, 1951.

A/C Judson West, Roxbury, Mass. Killed at T.A.A.F. in Jan. 1944.

Capt. George E. Gray, 809 McDowell St., Welch, W. Va. and 637 Keefer Pl. N. W., Washington, D. C. Missing in action in battle of Korea. Failed to return from a strafing in enemy territory on April 5, 1951.

S/Sgt. Kenneth Austin. Killed in an F-82 jet plane at the National Fighter Gunnery Meet in May 1949.

THE MEN—THE RECORDS

THE ORIGINAL 99th FIGHTER SQUADRON

Comanding Officer: Lieut. Colonel Benjamin O. Davis, Jr., Washington, D. C. (Pilot)

Operation Officer: Captain George Spencer Roberts, Fairmount, West Virginia (Pilot)

Assistant Operation Officer: Lieut. Erwin B. Lawrence, Cleveland, Ohio (Pilot)

Armament Officer: Lieut. William R. Thompson, Pittsburgh, Pennsylvania

Executive Officer: Lieut. Henry M. Letcher, Jr., Washington, D. C.

Engineering Officer: Lieut. Herbert Carter, Natchez, Mississippi

Provost Marshal & Intelligence Officer: Lieut. Cornelius Vincent, Boston, Massachusetts

Ordnance Officer: Lieut. George R. Curri, Los Angeles, California

Communication Officer: Lieut. Dudley W. Stevenson, Washington, D. C.

Assistant Intelligence Officer: Lieut. James L. Johnson, Washington, D. C.

Adjutant: Lieut. Bernard Proctor, Philadelphia, Pennsylvania

Adjutant: Captain Hayden C. Johnson, Washington, D. C.

Flight Surgeon: Captain Maurice C. Johnson, Washington, D. C.

Supply Officer: Lieut. Benote H. Wimp, Chicago, Illinois
Personnel Adjutant: Lieut. George Pettross, Washington, D. C.
Commanding Officer of service group attached to 99th: Captain
　　Elmer D. Jones, Washington, D. C.
Supply Officer of service group: Lieut. Thomas Malone, Detroit,
　　Michigan

Pilots:

Lieut. Lemuel R. Custis, Hartford, Connecticut
Lieut. Clarence Jamison, Cleveland, Ohio
Lieut. William A. Campbell, Tuskegee Institute, Alabama
Lieut. Charles B. Hall, Brazil, Indiana
Lieut. Paul G. Mitchell, Washington, D. C.
Lieut. Sidney P. Brooks, Cleveland, Ohio
Lieut. John W. Rogers, Chicago, Illinois
Lieut. Walter I. Lawson, Newton, Virginia
Lieut. James B. Knighten, Tulsa, Oklahoma
Lieut. Willie Ashley, Jr., Sumter, South Carolina
Lieut. George R. Bolling, Phoebus, Virginia
Lieut. Graham Smith, Ahoskie, North Carolina
Lieut. Louis R. Purnell, Snowhill, Maryland
Lieut. James Wiley, Pittsburgh, Pennsylvania
Lieut. Willie H. Fuller, Tarboro, North Carolina
Lieut. Spann Watson, Hackensack, New Jersey
Lieut. Lee Rayford, Ardwick, Maryland
Lieut. James McCullin, St. Louis, Missouri
Lieut. Sherman White, Montgomery, Alabama
Lieut. Samuel Bruce, Seattle, Washington
Lieut. Leon Roberts, Pritchard, Alabama

Enlisted Men
Airplane Mechanics:

M/Sgt. Clarence W. Clarke	S/Sgt. Charles Hensley
T/Sgt. Ralph E. Jackson	Sgt. Leon Coles
S/Sgt. Milton R. Brooks	S/Sgt. Leonard Calland
S/Sgt. Robert J. Chapman	M/Sgt. C. A. Bordeux
S/Sgt. Thomas E. Combs	Sgt. Robert Howard
S/Sgt. James Gary, Jr.	S/Sgt. Lawman Boykin

S/Sgt. Herman Jones
S/Sgt. Elliot W. Lucas
Sgt. Julius C. Lovett
Sgt. James A. Jackson
Corp. James A. Lockhart
S/Sgt. James Handy
Corp. Leonard Brower
S/Sgt. Alexander Crawford
S/Sgt. Ellsworth H. Dansby
S/Sgt. Earl D. Dillard
S/Sgt. Charles P. Feaster
S/Sgt. Glenn A. Garner

S/Sgt. Thomas Gill
Sgt. Alexton Boone, Jr.
T/Sgt. James Anderson, Jr.
Corp. John Turner
S/Sgt. Charles Davis
Sgt. Charles Ingram
S/Sgt. Joseph T. Hamilton
S/Sgt. Robert L. Smith
S/Sgt. William O. Warner
Corp. Paul E. Moss
(Armament)
(Parachute Rigger)

ORIGINAL 332nd FIGHTER GROUP

I HEADQUARTERS

Davis, Jr., Benjamin O., Lt. Col., AC, Commanding
Beck, Franklin B., Capt., DC, Dental Service
Brooks, Nelson S., Capt., AC, Executive
Marchbanks, Vance N., Jr., Capt., MC, Medical (Flight
Surgeon)
Perry, Cyrus W., Capt., CC, Chaplain
Banks, William A., 1st Lt., AC
Christmas, Joseph A., 1st Lt., AC
Harvey, Denzal T., 1st Lt., AC
Leonard, Wilmore B., 1st Lt., AC
McDaniel, Armour G., 1st Lt., AC
Money, Thomas J., 1st Lt., AC, Adjutant Personnel
Pitts, Robert G., 1st Lt., AC
Purnell, Louis R., 1st Lt., AC
Richardson, Roosevelt, 1st Lt., AC
Ross, Mac, 1st Lt., AC, Group Operation
Scurlock, Robert S., 1st Lt., AC
Ware, Ray B., 1st Lt., AC
Kelly, Jr., William A., 2nd Lt., AC
Richardson, Virgil J., 2nd Lt., AC

[215]

Simmons, Edward G., 2nd Lt., AC
Townsend, Prentice A., 2nd Lt., Ord., Ordnance
Womack, William M., 2nd Lt., AC
Edghill, Edward A., WOJO, AUS

OFFICERS: 100th Fighter Squadron
Anderson, Harry B., Capt., MC
Tresville, Robert B., Capt., AC, Commanding
Caesar, Richard C., 1st Lt., AC
Crockett, Woodrow W., 1st Lt., AC
Dickson, Lawrence E., 1st Lt., AC
Exum, Percy J., 1st Lt., Ord.
Jackson, Melvin T., 1st Lt., AC
Johnson, Morris T., 1st Lt., AC, Executive
Lumpkin, Theodore G., 1st Lt., AC
Mattison, William T., 1st Lt., AC, Asst. Operation
Pullam, Richard C., 1st Lt., AC
Quick, John B., 1st Lt., AC, Chaplain
Turner, Andrew D., 1st Lt., AC, Operation
Briggs, John F., 2nd Lt., AC
Bowman, Henry P., 2nd Lt., AC
Curtis, Samuel L., 2nd Lt., AC
Ellington, Spurgeon N., 2nd Lt., AC
Givings, Clemenceau, 2nd Lt., AC
Hopkins, Moses, 2nd Lt., AC
Hall, Richard W., 2nd Lt., AC
Holsclaw, Jack D., 2nd Lt., AC
Jefferson, Samuel, 2nd Lt., AC
Johnson, Langdon E., 2nd Lt., AC
McCreary, Walter L., 2nd Lt., AC
Moore, Theopolis D., 2nd Lt., AC
Morgan, Dempsey W., 2nd Lt., AC
Mosby, Milledge J., 2nd Lt., AC
Nelson, Robert H., Jr., 2nd Lt., AC
Norris, Lester S., 2nd Lt., AC
Palmer, Walter J. A., 2nd Lt., AC

[216]

Taylor, George A., 2nd Lt., AC
Steward, Lowell C., 2nd Lt., AC
Stoudmire, Norvell C., 2nd Lt., AC
Washington, Alexander, 2nd Lt., AC
Williams, Craig H., 2nd Lt., AC
Woods, Carrol S., 2nd Lt., AC
Woods, Williard L., 2nd Lt., AC
Wyatt, Beryl, 2nd Lt., AC
Wyatt, William C., 2nd Lt., AC

OFFICERS: 301st. Fighter Squadron
CAPTAIN
Debow, Charles H., AC, Commanding
1st Lts.
Byrd, Paul F., AC, Weather Officer
Daniels, Roland H., AC, Executive
Downs, Walter M., AC
Elsberry, Joseph D., AC
Govan, Claude B., AC
Rayford, Lee, AC, Operation
Scott, Samuel C., AC
Maples, Andrew, Jr., AC
Polkinghorne, James R., AC
Prowell, John R., AC
Waugh, Bascom S., MC, Flight Surgeon
Wilson, Commie, AC

2nd Lts.

Ballard, Alton F.	AC	Fuller, Samuel L.	AC
Browne, Gene C.	AC	Hatchett, Morris M.	AC
Cabiness, Marshall S.	AC	Jefferson, Lawrence B.	AC
Cisco, Arnold W.	AC	King, Robert L.	AC
Dooley, Lawrence C.	AC	Langston, Carroll N., Jr.	AC
Dunne, Charles A.	AC	Leahr, John H.	AC
Esters, Maurice V.	AC	McFatridge, James M.	AC
Foreman, Walter T.	AC	Lewis, Joe A.	AC
Faulkner, William J.	AC	Penn. Starling B.	AC

[217]

Rogers, Cornelius G.	AC	Turner, Leonard F.	AC
Sawyer, Harold E.	AC	Walker, Frank D.	AC
Taylor, Paulus C.	AC	Wiggins, Robert H.	AC
Taylor, Ulysses S.	AC	Williams, William F.	AC

OFFICERS: 302nd Squadron
CAPTAIN
Maloney, Arnold H., MC, Flight Surgeon
1st Lts.
Beverly, John R., AC
Brooks, Milton R., AC
Burton, Chester R., ORD
Bullock, Benjamin F., AC
Davis, Alfonso W., AC
Gleed, Edward C., AC, Commanding
Haywood, Vernon, AC
Pruitt, Wendell O., AC, Operation
Punch, Vernon E., AC
Sheppard, Harry A., AC
Spencer, Roy N., AC
Watson, Dudley N., AC
Weathers, Luke J., AC

2nd Lts.

Adams, Paul	AC	Lincoln, Vernon B.	AC
Archer, Lee A.	AC	McGee, Charles H.	AC
Blackwell, Hubron	AC	Melton, William R.	AC
Bussey, Charles N.	AC	Mohr, Dean B.	AC
Conley, James M.	AC	Moulden, William	AC
Green, William W., Jr.	AC	Romine, Roger	AC
Gordon, Elmer L.	AC	Smith, Edward N.	AC
Groves, Weldon K.	AC	Smith, Luther H., Jr.	AC
Haley, George J.	AC	Taylor, Elmer W.	AC
Hunter, Willie S.	AC	Walker, James A.	AC
Hutchins, Freddie	AC	Westmoreland, Walter	AC
Johnson, Everette W.	AC	Wilkins, Lawrence D.	AC
Kirkpatrick, Felix	AC		

[218]

EXTRA OFFICER PERSONNEL

2nd Lt. George E. Gray	AC
2nd Lt. Charles F. Jamerson	AC
2nd Lt. John S. Sloan	AC
2nd Lt. Alvin N. Temple	AC
2nd Lt. John Daniels	AC
2nd Lt. John J. Suggs	AC
2nd Lt. William R. Bartley	AC
2nd Lt. Harry J. Daniels	AC
2nd Lt. Joseph P. Gomer	AC
2nd Lt. Wayne V. Liggins	AC
2nd Lt. Clayborne A. Lockett	AC

REPLACEMENT PILOTS:
Alexander, Robert, 2nd Lt., AC
Alsbrook, William, 2nd Lt., AC
Barnes, Gentry E., 2nd Lt., AC
Bailey, Henry, 2nd Lt., AC
Bolden, Edgar L., 2nd Lt., AC
Bonan, Leonell H., 2nd Lt., AC
Bradford, Clarence, 2nd Lt., AC
Bratcher, Everett A., 2nd Lt., AC
Brooks, Milton R., Capt., AC
Caldwell, Langston H., 2nd Lt., AC
Carl, Carey, 2nd Lt., AC
Chandler, Robert C., 2nd Lt., AC
Charlton, Terry J., 2nd Lt., AC
Chineworth, Joseph, 2nd Lt., AC
Cox, Hannibal, Capt., AC
Cross, William, Jr., 2nd Lt., AC
Darnell, Charles E., 2nd Lt., AC
Dart, Clarence W., Jr., Capt., AC
Edwards, John E., 2nd Lt., AC
Edwards, William H., 2nd Lt., AC
Ellis, Carl F., 2nd Lt., AC
Ellis, William, 2nd Lt., AC

Fuller, Willie, 2nd Lt., AC
Gaines, Thurston L., 2nd Lt., AC
Garrison, Robert L., 2nd Lt., AC
Golden, Newman C., 2nd Lt., AC
Goodenough, Purnell J., 2nd Lt., AC
Gorham, Alfred M., 2nd Lt., AC
Gould, Cornelius, 2nd Lt., AC
Gray, Leo R., 2nd Lt., AC
Green, Paul I., 2nd Lt., AC
Greenlea, George B., 2nd Lt., AC
Harper, Samuel W., 2nd Lt., AC
Harris, Richard, 2nd Lt., AC
Halloman, William H., II, 2nd Lt., AC
Harder, Richard S., Capt., AC
Hill, Charles A., Jr., 2nd Lt., AC
Hudson, Lincoln, 2nd Lt., AC
Isles, George, 2nd Lt., AC
Johnson, Conrad A., 2nd Lt., AC
Johnson, Robert C., 2nd Lt., AC
Jones, Hubert, 2nd Lt., AC
Kimbrough, Benjamin R., 2nd Lt., AC
Knighten, James B., 2nd Lt., AC
Lacy, Hezekiah, 2nd Lt., AC
Lawrence, Robert W., 2nd Lt., AC
Lucas, Wendell, Capt., AC
Lyles, John H., 2nd Lt., AC
Lyles, Payton H., 2nd Lt., AC
Lynch, George A., 2nd Lt., AC
Lynch, Louis J., 2nd Lt., AC
Mann, Hiram, 2nd Lt., AC
Merriweather, Elbert N., 2nd Lt., AC
Mitchell, James, 2nd Lt., AC
Morris, Harold, 2nd Lt., AC
Murdie, Robert J., 2nd Lt., AC
Newman, Christopher, 2nd Lt., AC
O'Neal, Robert, 2nd Lt., AC

Oliphant, Clarence A., 2nd Lt., AC
Orduna, Ralph, 2nd Lt., AC
Payne, Turner W., 2nd Lt., AC
Pennington, Leland, 2nd Lt., AC
Peoples, Henry R., 2nd Lt., AC
Pillows, Robert A., Jr., 2nd Lt., AC
Porter, John H., 2nd Lt., AC
Rice, Price D., 2nd Lt., AC
Roberts, Leroy, Jr., 2nd Lt., AC
Robinson, Carroll, 2nd Lt., AC
Robinson, Curtis, 2nd Lt., AC
Ross, Washington D., 2nd Lt., AC
Saunders, Pearlee, 2nd Lt., AC
Scales, Norman W., 2nd Lt., AC
Schell, Wyrain T., 2nd Lt., AC
Scott, Henry B., 2nd Lt., AC
Selden, Wiley W., 2nd Lt., AC
Sherrod, Earle S., Jr., 2nd Lt., AC
Smith, Eugene, 2nd Lt., AC
Spann, Calvin J., 2nd Lt., AC
Stanton, Charles R., 2nd Lt., AC
Stewart, Nathaniel C., 2nd Lt., AC
Tate, Charles W., 2nd Lt., AC
Thompson, Reed E., 2nd Lt., AC
Verwayne, Peter C., 2nd Lt., AC
Washington, Samuel L., 2nd Lt., AC
Watts, Samuel, 2nd Lt., AC
Wheeler, Jimmie D., 2nd Lt., AC
White, Harold, 2nd Lt., AC
White, Joseph, 2nd Lt., AC
Whitney, Yenwith K., 2nd Lt., AC
Whittaker, Peter A., 2nd Lt., AC
Williams, Lawrence, 2nd Lt., AC
Williams, Robert W., 2nd Lt., AC
Wilson, Theodore A., 2nd Lt., A
Wilson, Bertram W., Jr., 2nd Lt., AC

[221]

Wilson, James A., 2nd Lt., AC
Wilson, Myron, 2nd Lt., AC
Wright, Hiram, 2nd Lt., AC
Wright, Kenneth, 2nd Lt., AC
Young, Albert L., 2nd Lt., AC

FOOTNOTES

CHAPTER I

[1] Record of Public Relations Office, Tuskegee Army Air Field.

[2] Hastie, William H., *On Clipped Wings,* Published by National Association for the Advancement of Colored People. New York, Oct. 1943, p. 5.

[3] Ibid.

[4] Ibid.

[5] Ibid, p. 13.

[6] Release No. N-3—Selective Service Headquarters, Washington, D. C., March 25, 1944.

CHAPTER II

[1] Colonel Benjamin O. Davis, Jr., Press Conference at Pentagon on September 10, 1943.

CHAPTER V

[1] Pyle, Ernie, *Brave Men,* New York, 1944, P. 16, Copyright, 1944, by Henry Holt & Co.

[2] Ibid. p. 20.

CHAPTER VI

[1] Pyle, Ernie, *Brave Men,* Henry Holt & Co., New York, 1944, p. 161.

[2] Ringold, Herbert H., "Salerno," *Air Force*, April, 1944, pp. 28-35. U. S. Govt. Printing Office, Wash., D. C.

[3] Ibid.

[4] Dean, Fred M., Col. "The Luftwaffe at Bay," *Air Force,* Oct., 1943, pp. 6-7 and 56.

[5] Time Magazine, Sept. 20, 1943.

CHAPTER VII

[1] Matthews, Herbert L., "Road of Mud, Fatigue, and Glory," *New York Times,* Dec. 26, 1943.

[2] Pyle, Ernie, *Brave Men,* Copyright, 1944, by Henry Holt & Co., New York, 1944, p. 233.

CHAPTER VIII

[1] Norstad, Lauris, Brig. Gen., "Airlock in Italy," *Air Force,* January 1945, pp. 31-36. U. S. Govt. Printing Office, Wash., D. C.

[2] *Second Report of Commanding General of the Army Air Forces to the Secretary of War,* Feb. 27, 1945, pp. 45-46. U. S. Govt. Printing Office, Wash., D. C.

[3] Norstad, op. cit. p. 35.

CHAPTER XII

[1] Norstad, Lauris, Brig. Gen. "Airlock in Italy," *Air Force,* January, 1945, pp. 31-35. U. S. Govt. Printing Office, Wash., D. C.

CHAPTER XIV

[1] Commager, Henry Steele, *The Story of the Second World War.* Little Brown & Co., Boston, 1945, p. 438.

CHAPTER XVIII

[1] Eisenhower, Dwight D., *Crusade in Europe,* p. 410 Copyright 1948, by Doubleday & Company, Inc., New York.

CHAPTER XXI

[1] Hastie, William H., *On Clipped Wings,* Published by National Association for the Advancement of Colored People, New York, Oct., 1943, p. 19.

CHAPTER XXII

[1] Ebony Magazine, Oct., 1952, p. 22.

[2] Afro-American, Oct. 31, 1950.

[3] Afro-American, Nov. 28, 1950.

[4] Ebony Magazine, Oct. 1950, p. 25.

REFERENCES:

Eisenhower, Dwight D. *Crusade in Europe.* Doubleday & Co., Inc. 1948. Garden City, New York.

Commager, Henry Steele. *The Story of the Second World War.* Little, Brown & Co., 1945. Boston, Mass.

Gentile, Don S. *One Man Air Force.* L. B. Fischer Publishing Corp. N. Y.

Hastie, William H. *On Clipped Wings.* National Association for the Advancement of Colored People, Oct. 1943. New York.

Lind, Ragnor G., *The Falcon—Combat Story of the 79th Fighter Group.* F. Bruckman, Munich, Germany, 1946.

McInnis, Edgar. *The War, 5th Year*. Oxford University Press, New York, 1945.

Murray, Florence. *The Negro Handbook*. Current Reference Publications, N. Y., 1944.

Pyle, Ernie. *Brave Men*. Henry Holt & Co., New York, 1944.

Second Report of the Commanding General of the Army Air Forces to the Secretary of War—February 27, 1945. U. S. Govt. Printing Office, Washington, D. C.

Third Report of the Commanding General of the Army Air Forces to the Secretary of War—November 12, 1945. U. S. Govt. Printing Office, Washington, D. C.

Special Orders of Tuskegee Army Air Field—1941-1946.

Special Order No. 338, Selfridge Field, Michigan—20 Dec. 1943.

Letter. *Records of the 99th Fighter Squadron*, U.S.A.F., History: Research: Library Division, Maxwell Air Base, Alabama.

War Department Bureau of Public Relations Releases—1941-1946.

Biographical Survey—Pilots of the 99th Fighter Squadron and the 332nd Fighter Group.

Personal Interviews—Members of the 99th Fighter Squadron and the 332nd Fighter Group.

Temple Alva, Captain—*Diary* (unpublished)

Thomas, Edward, Captain—*Diary* (unpublished)

NEWSPAPERS & PERIODICALS

Afro-American—1941-1951

Pittsburgh Courier—1941-1951

Norfolk Journal and Guide—1941-1951

New York Times, 1942

Time Magazine—Sept., 1943

Air Force—1942-1946

The Lantern—May 27, 1949 (Lockbourne Air Force Base, Columbus, Ohio.)

Wings over Tuskegee—Tuskegee Institute release.

[225]